THE TRUTH ABOUT MORTGAGES

THE TRUTH ABOUT
MORTGAGES

How to Make the Most
of Your Borrowing Power

Alberta Cefis
&
Roberta Hague

KEY PORTER BOOKS

To Alberto and Giovanna Cefis, my parents,
for the adventure of life   AGC

To Tim, Britton, and Dyson, "my boys"   RLH

Library and Archives Canada Cataloguing in Publication

Cefis, Alberta

The truth about mortgages: how to make the most of your borrowing power / Alberta Cefis and Roberta Hague. — Rev. ed.

Includes index.

ISBN 1-55263-684-4

1. Mortgage loans—Canada. I. Hague, Roberta II. Title.

HG2040.5.C2C43 2005   332.7'2'0971   C2004-907025-8

THE CANADA COUNCIL | LE CONSEIL DES ARTS
FOR THE ARTS | DU CANADA
SINCE 1957 | DEPUIS 1957

ONTARIO ARTS COUNCIL
CONSEIL DES ARTS DE L'ONTARIO

The publisher gratefully acknowledges the support of the Canada Council for the Arts and the Ontario Arts Council for its publishing program. We acknowledge the support of the Government of Ontario through the Ontario Media Development Corporation's Ontario Book Initiative.

We acknowledge the financial support of the Government of Canada through the Book Publishing Industry Development Program (BPIDP) for our publishing activities.

Key Porter Books Limited
Six Adelaide Street East, Tenth Floor
Toronto, Ontario
Canada M5C 1H6
www.keyporter.com

Text design: Jack Steiner
Electronic formatting: Heidy Lawrance Associates

Printed and bound in Canada

05 06 07 08 09 6 5 4 3 2

Contents

Foreword

Canada is a nation of borrowers. And while six in ten Canadians agreed with the statement in our poll on the topic for this publication that "being in debt scares me," nine out of ten of us borrow. After all, without borrowing, most of us would never be able to own our homes or lead the lives to which we aspire. So much so that three-quarters of Canadians acknowledge that they consider their debt payments to simply be part of their day-to-day living expenses.

Naturally, Canadians want to pay down their borrowing. But while over 80 percent of those who borrow say they have a *definite plan* on how they're going to repay their debt, they're not particularly effective about the way they borrow—tending to accumulate debt in a relatively haphazard way. In fact, as a nation of consumers, our debt management methods are a bit suspect.

Most Canadians will admit that they've put off the purchase of something they say they've needed until they had the money. But we also know that for all those purchases that were deferred, there were lots of others that weren't. For many, it's tough to be prudent when the need, want, or desire is immediate.

And while six in ten Canadians say they've taken steps to reduce their borrowing on high-interest credit cards, and the same number say they've reduced the number of credit cards in their wallet, half of Canadians acknowledge they have not structured their debt so they pay the lowest possible amount of interest. Clearly, as a nation of credit users and debt financers, we could use some help.

This becomes even more evident when you look at just *when* Canadians hope they'll be debt-free. Not surprisingly, the average debt-free target age becomes higher with each age group—like climbing a ladder, with new steps added at the top every few years. Cars, housing, children, post-secondary education, a cottage, vacations—these are just some of the things in the life cycle that make life and debt go hand in hand for most. Our polling shows that on average, people who are 30 think they will be able to live debt-free by the time they reach 45. By the time they're 45, they have pushed off their debt-free target to age 56. Regardless of their level of affluence or comfort with debt, Canadians generally hope to be debt-free by the time they reach their early 50s.

Clearly, wishing and hoping just aren't enough to make our debt disappear.

And then there is the ultimate question of *how* to reduce the debt. More than half of Canadians believe that it would help if a financial institution would review our total debt load and suggest how we can get ahead. This book is written for you.

Ipsos-Reid has been conducting research on Canadian consumers and their borrowing habits on behalf of many of Canada's financial lending institutions for 23 years. In addition, we've produced annual debt, housing, and mortgage studies over the last decade that have become national hallmarks. And, through these studies we've developed considerable consumer insight, with perspectives on the motivations, expectations, and behaviours of Canadians. We've examined how values, attitudes, and expectations have played out in this nation of borrowers.

We have been privileged to work with Scotiabank on studies that cover important ground on the issue of consumer debt and borrowing. We're delighted to see our colleagues at Scotiabank take a broad and integrated view of homeownership and borrowing. They've shared valuable advice that will help Canadians get out from under the angst of borrowing and guide them to options and solutions that could not only help them realize their dreams and aspirations today, but live in comfort and contentment in the years to come.

John Wright
Senior Vice-President, Ipsos-Reid

Introduction

Over the course of a lifetime, most Canadians will negotiate several mortgages and personal loans. As bankers who have worked in personal finance for twenty years, we have seen many people follow their dreams. With the help of a mortgage, one couple was able to buy back the family cottage when they saw a For Sale sign go up. Another man financed the purchase of a motor home with a personal loan so that he and his wife could spend their retirement exploring the country, from the Cabot Trail to the Yukon. We've also counselled people who felt overwhelmed by the size of their mortgage. Or young people who, instead of celebrating their university graduation, were distressed at the size of their student loan. The delighted and despairing have one thing in common: they all borrowed money, a lot of money.

The other thing these people had in common was that they could have been savvier in their borrowing strategies, and ultimately more comfortable. What does that mean? Really, it's simple. The man who bought the motor home was so happy to be approved for the loan, he never thought about whether there might have been a better way to finance the purchase. He missed the opportunity to make the most of his borrowing power, and we're not referring to negotiating the best interest rate. It's much more than that.

The Truth About Mortgages is designed to guide you through your life as a borrower and a homeowner, to give you greater insight into the decision-making process, and to equip you with useful tools to demystify it. Banks and other lenders are making great strides in sharing information about borrowing and presenting it in ways that are easy to understand. Information is more and more accessible directly over the Internet, including credit bureau information. Your challenge now is to make the most of this increasing transparency.

It's easy to feel overwhelmed by the process of applying for a mortgage or a line of credit. There's a lot at stake—a home for your family, for example—which increases your level of anxiety. Everyone dreads being judged or rejected on the basis of personal financial information. In the past, the decision-making process seemed mysterious and complicated. But now, with all the information available to you, you don't have to apply for credit without having a pretty good idea of the outcome.

At the heart of this book is the view of your home as an investment. It's not only your residence, but also probably the biggest investment you'll ever make. We'll look at how you can protect this investment and how to use it to be a better borrower. We'll offer guidance on how to navigate through important elements of the mortgage process. (We're assuming that if you have the cash to buy a house without a mortgage, then you're probably not reading this book!)

Who would benefit from *The Truth About Mortgages*? All those who suspect they could be better borrowers but don't know how. All those who feel uncomfortable borrowing money and those who never even consider their level of debt, not to mention the cost of it. And those who wonder how they'll manage their cash flow this month. More specifically, if you are struggling with student debt after graduation, a car loan that is taking forever to pay off, or the down payment on your first home, this book is for you. If you have borrowed money or expect to for any reason and have no idea how you'll pay it back, then this is absolutely required reading. If you're planning to buy a home or you already own a home—even if you don't owe a penny on it and have burned your mortgage papers—the book is still for you. If you have two or three children, like the average Canadian family, and they're all bright teenagers hoping to attend university, this book will help.

When we scanned the shelves of local bookstores recently, we observed a wealth of new books on investing, but only a limited number of titles on borrowing, mortgages, and homeownership—and what *was* available was written by Americans for Americans. Here, we offer you a uniquely Canadian perspective, reflecting Canadian values and culture, Canadian taxes and regulatory context, and Canadian service providers. So please don't rely on an American expert or your brother-in-law from Ohio for advice!

In the first chapter of this book, we explore our ever-increasing appetite for borrowing. We'll tackle the myths and misperceptions arising from out-of-date sources of information. And we'll focus on the truths about borrowing (debt and credit) in this marketplace.

You might wonder what outcome you can expect if you read *The Truth About Mortgages*. Overall, you'll feel better. The book provides you with some simple strategies to help you more comfortably manage your borrowing. You will have insight into the best ways to use your borrowing options. You'll better understand how to reduce your borrowing costs. You'll be more capable of organizing your borrowing so that you can get out from under the burden of constant anxiety. You'll find the solutions that best fit your personal goals and your comfort zone.

You'll understand if you are ready for that next big step. Whether it's a retirement property in the country or a loft in the city, you'll be faced with some basic questions: Are you ready to buy a home? What type of home can you afford? Will it be a condominium, a townhouse, or a detached house?

Centrally located in the city or in the suburbs? Or maybe you're thinking of buying a cottage, a ski chalet, or a cabin deep in the woods. If you already own a home, you'll understand the pivotal role that homeownership plays in your investment portfolio.

Stop worrying (a fruitless, energy-draining activity!) and focus on your dreams and passions. We all know the old saying that life is too short. And it's true. We watch our children grow up all too quickly, and we watch as our dreams fade. We have a tendency to avoid active participation in our own financial lives; it's not that we can't make decisions, it's just that we're fearful of debt and too busy with the rest of our lives to get off the fence and deal with our emerging financial needs and desires. Well, we're going to help get you off the fence and on your feet, secure in the knowledge that you can achieve a better borrowing position.

With the prime rate at its lowest level in more than 40 years and fixed-term mortgage rates at their lowest in 50 years, we're enjoying the benefit of a unique position in history. At the same time, we have been facing a growing mountain of debt as the economy has struggled through an industry-led downturn and the second-worst bear market in a hundred years. Still, consumer spending has kept the Canadian economy chugging along. In light of these good times for consumers, now might be the right time to reflect on what we need to do to ensure our financial security. If you commit to reading these pages, we'll make it worth your while. We won't have all the answers here, but we will ease some stress. We'll laugh together. And maybe we'll even surprise you. Hold on. Here we go.

CHAPTER 1

Dispelling the Myths

Karen has several credit cards and they all carry a large balance. She makes monthly payments on each card that average a little more than the minimum and pays the balances off in full once a year, when she gets a bonus at work.

Karen is exactly like most of us. Sure, we're supposed to pay off the cards every month, we know that. Just like we're supposed to eat lots of vegetables and get good exercise. (We're actually better about doing that.) So what's the point of this book? No, this isn't just another financial-planning guide that will tell you to keep those credit cards paid in full. We want you to have some fun learning how to find your comfort zone and become a better borrower. Like most Canadians, you've accumulated some debt over the years. After all, let's face it: debt is a fact of life. Or at least it is for most people. Unless you call it "credit," in which case you have that too!

In consumer research over the past twenty years, people have told the "good debt/bad debt" story over and over. "Credit is good until it turns into debt," they say. While there is some truth to the observation, it's not entirely correct. It's true that Canadians can and do distinguish good debt from bad. We know that bad debt is what you borrow, for which you have nothing to show. Good debt is what you borrow to acquire an appreciating asset. (By the way, not all bad debt is on credit cards, and credit cards don't have to be bad.) Now we're going to look at how using your home equity can really improve your borrowing position.

Currently, Canadians have debts totalling more than $800 billion. Three-quarters of that is in mortgages, with the other quarter in personal lines of credit, loans, and credit cards. Fuelled by low interest rates and rising real estate values, borrowing has increased more than 20% in just the past two years, and the highest area of growth has been in personal lines of credit, particularly home-equity-secured lines, which have become a flexible and cost-efficient borrowing facility. Still, while many Canadians have been paying off high-cost borrowing with lower-cost alternatives, the overall growth rate has been staggering.

You have probably contributed your fair share to that growth in consumer credit and from time to time reflect, with perhaps a touch of anxiety, on your personal level of debt. Relax. We're going to acknowledge how much debt you have, debunk a few myths, and help you to be a better borrower.

Let us introduce you to a few people we know. They are each at a quite different place in life and so exemplify a number of different situations:

Karen, who appeared at the beginning of this chapter, is a 32-year-old account executive at a Vancouver ad agency. She loves her life, which includes a close-knit extended family and a circle of friends who, like Karen, are well-educated and outgoing. She is about to get a big promotion, and she feels her career is taking off.

Karen rents a pleasant apartment in a lovely old building overlooking English Bay. She would like to buy a condo, but real estate prices in Vancouver are astronomical. She watches her friends getting married and buying houses. Karen considers her mountain bike her biggest asset and her line of credit a symbol of success, but wonders if there is any way she will ever own a home on her own.

Maria and John are a couple in their early 30s who met in university and married when they graduated. They live in Toronto with their four-year-old daughter and two-year-old twin boys. Maria and John were surprised, delighted, and anxious when they first learned they were going to have twins. Their house in the city was rather small and so they moved to a large new suburban home, which still afforded them easy access by car to John's work. Maria's parents are Portuguese immigrants; John's parents are also immigrants, but of mixed European heritage. Maria and John knew they would need lots of family support; their new home, while it does put a strain on their budget, is closer to their extended families. Also, it's in a neighbourhood filled with young families. They knew they had found a good fit.

Maria had gone back to work when their daughter was six months old, but three children meant expensive day care—more money than the couple could afford. So after a chat with their personal banking manager, Maria and John made some big financial decisions. They decided that Maria would quit her job and stay at home to care for the "double blessing." At the same time, they had to replace one of their old cars for a more reliable new car for John to travel into the city for work. They are still a bit stretched with all the expenses they have incurred recently, but with a bit of time and some help, they will be on very strong footing.

John runs his own small business, a cleaning services company. He pays the household bills and together they are very careful about expenditures.

Alya and Sandor are both married for the second time. Her family is from the Middle East. His is from Eastern Europe, and lightning flashes whenever their families get together. She is 47. He is 53. They live in Montreal.

Alya has two children from her former marriage, both in their early twenties, one in medical school and the other studying architecture; they live in apartments with classmates. Sandor has four children in their late twenties and thirties, all well established. Three are living in or near Montreal. Sandor's eldest son is married and lives in Ottawa with his young family; they visit Montreal often. Between them, Alya and Sandor have seven siblings spread across Europe and North America, with lots of nieces and nephews with whom they communicate often via e-mail.

Sandor owns a car dealership. Alya is the CFO of a mid-size bakery business. The entire family operates easily in English and French, but Alya is also fluent in Farsi, having spent her childhood years in Iran. Sandor is fluent in Hungarian. They enjoy the arts and love to travel. By any measure, they are successful financially, but they have had some big expenses getting children through university, and their narrow old row house seems to require regular (and expensive) repair.

And, while Sandor thinks he's managing the family's money, in fact they share responsibility for paying their bills. Alya directs a bit of money each month, when she can, into an RRSP, since neither she nor her husband has a pension plan. They are aware of the need to plan for their retirement, which still seems a bit remote, but not all that far off. They are beginning to wonder if the house that has served them well for the past few years is perhaps a bit small to accommodate visits from their extended family. And those stairs will be daunting as they get older.

All of these acquaintances have been working on their debts based on one or two myths. We have heard stories about people who got into trouble with their borrowing; many of these stories perpetuate ideas about "bad debt." Misperceptions, based on historical truths that are no longer relevant, are also at play here. For example, well-intentioned advice from parents and grand-parents who bought their last home 30 or 40 years ago, may not serve you well today.

What do we mean? A colleague recently told us about an ad she had seen on TV. A woman is making jam in her kitchen, and when asked why she turns the jars upside down, she acknowledges that she has absolutely no idea, but that's the way her mother bottled jam, and her mother before her. You get the idea.

It's hard to break out of the mould. We all have personal accounts of advice (solicited or unsolicited) from our parents, neighbours, friends—advice that is rooted in generations of tradition. As a result, what may have been entirely appropriate at an earlier time is carried on forever, or at least until new knowledge from a more current source can take us in a new direction.

Let's look at those jam jars again. In fact, many people successfully seal their jam jars by turning them upside down. But while this may be an expedient approach, it's not the best, in that the seal is not very strong, leading to spoilage before you can enjoy your effort. A more generally recommended approach to sealing jars is to use boiling water, which can achieve a much better seal, ensuring your jams and other preserves are safe for at least a year. As well, the boiling-water approach is safer than the paraffin-wax option some of us remember from the kitchens of our youth.

So here are the key messages in a few myths we've heard. Do any of these pieces of advice sound familiar?

1. "Paying off your mortgage is good."
   "Paying off your mortgage is bad."

2. "Pay into your RRSP before you pay down your mortgage."
   "Pay down your mortgage before you pay into your RRSP."

3. "Real estate is a great investment."
   "Real estate is the worst investment you can make."

4. "If interest rates go up, you'll lose your home."
   "If interest rates go up, don't worry, you'll be fine."

5. "Pay off your credit cards first."
   "Keep your credit cards active to preserve your credit rating."

You're starting to get the picture: there is no single position that applies to everyone, and there is some truth in all these observations. Your situation is as unique as your personal goals, experiences, opportunities, and patterns of behaviour. Remember that the advice you get is often based on the unique personal experience of the person offering it.

While there is no single answer, there are some overarching principles to keep in mind. Let's look at these one at a time. By doing so, we'll help get you closer to homeownership, and then debt-free.

1. Paying off your mortgage is important. And it's the right thing to do as long as it's the last and lowest-cost borrowing you have. We have seen too many people celebrate paying off their mortgage, even have friends and neighbours over for a barbecue to watch them burn their mortgage documents in a splendid ceremony. And they do this while carrying a car loan

and a $10,000 credit card balance! In fact, using your income and savings to pay off your mortgage completely is not the best way to go if you still have high-cost debt; as a general rule, mortgage debt has the lowest interest rate. Pay off the high-cost debt before you pay off the mortgage. Then you'll really have something to celebrate!

2. Pay into your RRSP or mortgage? Let's make this the final word on the age-old question that so many families have confronted every year for the past thirty years, ever since RRSPs were introduced in Canada. Do we make an RRSP contribution or a pre-payment on the mortgage this year? For most people, most of the time, in most situations, the answer is simple: first make the RRSP contribution, then take any tax refund generated by the RRSP contribution and use it to make a pre-payment on the mortgage. Generally, in a low-interest-rate environment, contributing to your RRSP will put you ahead. Now, when would it not make sense? Probably only if interest rates are rising and you won't be able to cope easily with increased mortgage payments when the mortgage term comes up for renewal. Consider your tax situation carefully. Why not make an RRSP contribution and get CCRA (Canada Customs and Revenue Agency) to generate a tax refund that you can use to reduce your mortgage?

     Another answer to this dilemma is to put your mortgage into a self-directed RRSP. With this approach, you end up paying the mortgage interest to yourself. But you need enough contribution room in your RRSP to include the entire value of your mortgage, and so this is not an option for everyone. We discuss the option a little more in Chapter 4.

3. Real estate can be a great investment. The value of the investment depends on your time horizon and how you plan to use the property. To make real estate a good investment, you really need to think long-term. It will obviously be a better investment if it is your primary residence, so that gains in value can accrue tax-free. On the other hand, many people who have income as a primary objective in their investments, along with growth of capital value, find that owning property that can be rented out to generate a monthly stream of income works well.

4. The interest-rate question is becoming a more pressing concern since we are at historically low interest-rate levels and there is room for rates to rise. Again, how well you can cope in an environment of rising rates depends on your personal situation. Can you handle $100 more in interest payments each month? On a line of credit with a balance of $75,000 at 5.5% today, it would take an interest-rate rise of 1.65% to 7.15% to

increase payments by that much. If your cash flow is very sensitive to rises in interest rates, then lock into a longer term to secure your payment. By the time your term matures, you will likely have had some increase in your income to cope with the larger payments. Only you know your sensitivity, so discuss your needs with your lender to ensure that you have a borrowing strategy that's right for you.

5. Not all credit cards are created equally. You'll often hear the blanket advice "Pay off your credit cards first." That assumes that all credit cards are high-rate vehicles for borrowing. It's true that many are, but not all. So the better advice is to pay off your higher-interest borrowing or trade it in for lower-cost alternatives. If you have a credit card charging 19% interest, can you convert it to a lower-rate card or line of credit? If you have unsecured borrowing, can you convert it to home-equity-secured borrowing, which is generally the best-priced form of borrowing available, whether in a term mortgage or a secured line of credit? By taking $10,000 from higher-rate cards and reducing your annual interest rate by 5%, you can save $500 every year. If you lower the rate by moving from a 19% card to a line of credit at 7%, you'll save $100 every month in carrying costs. So it's not about credit cards being a problem; it's the interest rate you're paying. Some credit cards are available at very attractive rates similar to rates of personal lines of credit, so look closely at your own borrowing. Don't just stick your head in the sand and ignore what you're paying. Be informed and use the best credit card and other borrowing vehicles to meet your needs, whether you want reward points, insurance features, or a better interest rate.

Let's dispel a few other misperceptions and explain some things that you, as a borrower, may benefit from knowing (we have also listed basic definitions in the Glossary at the end of the book):

- "Don't pay a cent for two years." If you're buying furniture or appliances from a retailer who gives you the option of not paying for a year or two, check the fine print so that you're not surprised by a huge balloon payment to cover the interest all at once. There can also be big fees attached to these payment-deferral arrangements. Some of these deals are great; others can cost you a lot. So ask up front about all the fees and charges and payments, and read the terms and conditions carefully for yourself. If there is something you don't understand, ask.
- "The first six months at an incredibly low rate." Well, if it *is* incredible, it's not sustainable. So you eventually pay one way or another; the issue is

how you pay and when. Does the interest rate jump after a few months? Are there high annual fees charged to the account? When you look at these early-rate offers, it helps to understand what APR means. It's an acronym for Annual Percentage Rate, which is the average annual rate of interest applied to your borrowing over the term of the borrowing, including fees and other costs. Always ask your lender for the APR so that you can understand the full cost of your borrowing.

- Making payments by the due date is your most important responsibility as a borrower. Lots of people want to know how many times they can be late on payments before it will affect their credit. There is no specific answer to that, and every lender can report payment delinquency differently. With some lenders, if you are just one day late with one payment, it will appear on your credit report. Others will wait until you are 30 days late, and maybe even wait until that has happened a few times. Bottom line, one late payment won't destroy your credit rating. Ten late payments sure will. Five late payments would have some impact, the extent of which could vary. Payment history is stored and reported in your credit report history for at least three years. So, if you're anticipating new borrowing needs on the horizon, make your payments consistently and on time. Even just the minimum payments will keep you in good standing.

- Having one lender pay out debt held by another lender should not affect your credit rating. It will only appear as a "payout" on your credit report. For all that anyone knows, you made the payment yourself. So if you can get one lender to provide you with a lower-rate borrowing solution, then get that lender to pay out your other borrowing and close that account.

- A credit counselling service (available through Credit Counselling Canada) can be very helpful if you're getting into difficulty and not able to meet your minimum payment obligations. The agencies that form Credit Counselling Canada are accredited and operate on a not-for-profit basis. A counsellor can help you work through what may seem like an impossible situation, especially if collection agencies are on your tail. If you do get to this stage, the situation will likely be reported to the credit bureau and thus alert future lenders. They'll see that you have had difficulty in the past and may refuse to grant you credit in the future. It will also mean that you'll pay more to offset the lender's anticipated risk, so it's always best to manage your borrowing carefully to avoid this situation.

- Protecting your credit rating is more important than ever. Pricing on your borrowing is increasingly attached to your credit risk profile. *Risk-based pricing* is used to establish the interest rate you will pay for your borrowing, and so this pricing is based on your credit risk profile when you establish the account. With revolving credit (credit cards and lines of credit), *performance-based pricing* is becoming more standard and your interest rate will be adjusted up if you are late making payments or don't meet the minimum payments. With performance-based pricing, your account would be restored from a high premium rate to a standard or preferred rate once you have achieved a period of consistent repayment.

Much more information on how credit ratings work appears in Chapter 7. It's crucial to understand credit ratings, and we're giving the subject a good bit of attention, since your credit rating is a key to being able to realize your dreams of homeownership. But let's move elsewhere for now and start with a better understanding of why we feel the way we do and the resulting behaviours. Only when we start with a bit of personal reflection will we be armed with the insight and knowledge to make some needed changes to our borrowing strategies.

CHAPTER 2

The Values and Attitudes That Drive Us

Before we look at borrowing patterns, let's examine why we do what we do. Here is the basic hypothesis:

Aspirations, combined with values and attitudes, plus our experiences, expectations, and opportunities, will together determine our behaviour.

How has this cultural framework evolved over time?

If you were born and raised in Canada, then chances are your teachers or your parents or grandparents quoted Shakespeare and Benjamin Franklin to you on the subject of borrowing. Do either of the following sound familiar?

"Neither a borrower nor a lender be,
For loan oft loses both itself and friend"

"He that goes a borrowing goes a sorrowing."

The first quote is from William Shakespeare's *Hamlet*, where Polonius is offering advice to his son, Laertes, who is setting out for France. This is the same fatherly speech in which Polonius counsels his son, "This above all: to thine own self be true." The second quote is from Benjamin Franklin, the great American statesman and economist, who declared that the way to wealth depends largely on hard work and frugality.

Many of us had families who coached us about how to save. And the media has dished up lots of advice on how to invest. Bookstore shelves overflow with books advocating different investment strategies. But the message we get on borrowing is basically "Don't do it unless you really have to." Rarely is there advice on how to be an effective borrower. That would actually require acknowledgement that we *are* borrowers. And that would involve a discussion of money. Many of us don't feel comfortable discussing the price of things (except when we find a really good bargain). In fact, we are more likely to talk about sex than money. Yet, the reality is that most of us borrow, at least at some point in our lives, and borrowing is not a bad thing in itself. It's how it's done, and how it's managed that makes all the difference.

Michael Adams, a leading researcher on Canadian values, asserts in his book *Better Happy Than Rich?*, "The money taboo persists: fully one-fifth of Canadians admit that they would be upset if their friends knew how much money they earn, and one-quarter would be upset if their co-workers knew." Adams points out that our social values and our financial behaviour are intimately connected. So looking at how our values and behaviour have changed may give us a better appreciation of why we do what we do, and why we feel the way we feel, and what we might be able to do to become better borrowers.

Now, let's take this insight on our values and consider how it relates to our approach to borrowing and homeownership. First, we'll look back at the postwar setting of the late 1940s and early 1950s. Canadians admired frugality. They worked hard to save for their homes. The community rallied around newly married couples to help them set up their first home, and people hoped to afford a radio in their living room. Homeownership was still a relatively new idea in North America, the result of the democratization of land ownership here, combined with old-fashioned hard work.

In those years, a mortgage was most often provided by a finance company—few of which exist today. Scotiabank first offered personal loans in Canada in 1958. It was only in 1967 that the *Bank Act* allowed banks to compete in the mortgage market in a significant way. The old expression "a mortgage is a mortgage is a mortgage" is probably rooted in those times, when really only one type of mortgage was available: one with a long-term, fixed rate and fixed payment plan, whether you borrowed from a finance company or from your parents. Families tended to have one income earner and set their expectations to that level. The Great Depression was still recent enough that the experience of economic hardship, combined with overarching social values, compelled you to work hard to save enough money before you bought something. This was the heyday of deferred gratification.

How times have changed! We're living in a consumer society. While those old core values prevail in your conscience, they are generally ignored when you see something you want. We make the purchase, feel anxious, and expect we'll figure out later how to pay for it. One of our branch managers was telling us recently about a couple who had just bought the home of their dreams in a central Ontario community. Just a few months later, they were in her office in tears, feeling overwhelmed by their mortgage. They should have felt jubilant about their home, but the doubts their families expressed had made them anxious. After a chat about good debt and bad debt and a review of their cash flow, the young couple recognized that they were living well within their means, in fact, were even saving! They left with smiles, their confidence restored.

Since our parents' or grandparents' generation, there has been a significant shift in attitudes towards borrowing. Earlier generations of Canadians maintained that you should save your money and make purchases only when you had the cash in hand. In a recent round of market research, consumers talked about how their parents "valued austerity" and cautioned them to be patient, saying, "You'll have what you want, in time." The baby boomers, however, were not so willing to defer gratification. We often hear comments like "Why not? You only live once!" or "Everyone uses credit. It's a part of life." Yet, while our expectations and attitudes about borrowing have changed, we are still tormented by the old, but prevailing values.

What are the reasons for such a profound change in our values over the generations? Or have the *core* values really changed? It's essentially our *aspirations* that have evolved, along with our experience and expectations. Television has had a lot to do with making us aware of the many advances in technology—smaller but increasingly multifunctional cellphones are a good example—feeding our appetite for greater conveniences in our lives. Our *values* have not moved much on the question of borrowing; more than three-quarters of Canadians agree that it is "very important" to pay down debts. So now we live in a paradigm where our values are in stark conflict with our experience and expectations.

Our aspirations shifted gradually from the post-war focus on "more for my children" to, in the 1970s, wanting "personal freedom." By the 1980s the boomers wanted "more for me." Then as women took on more senior roles in the workforce over the past twenty-plus years, there is more talk about "balance" and "simplification." Lately, the focus has shifted to "appreciation of what we have" and the need to feel "safe and secure." Our changing experience has clearly contributed to changing dreams and goals. Overall, Canadians place high importance on non-financial goals such as health and relationships.

Let's look more closely at the evolving role of women in our culture, and how that evolution has increased our expectations and affected borrowing. While it's true that women have always worked, either inside or outside the home, it was not until the last quarter of the twentieth century that their income became integral to the household cash flow. This is a huge shift—from "vacation savings" to core earnings that support the household. Consequently, there are higher expectations on a per-household basis and greater demand for conveniences.

With the growth in two-income households, the single-family dwelling has become more affordable. And everyone wants the newest and most efficient appliances. Even with double incomes, we still need to borrow to acquire these conveniences and have the home we want, plus two cars, not to mention good education for our children. Quality of life is the priority, and unlike our grandparents, we'll borrow to get it. Since *time* is the one thing that is not in abundance in the modern household, some argue that we are compelled to buy the conveniences to achieve quality of life.

Another big change over the generations is the onslaught of "service providers," who are ready and more than willing to help us borrow to achieve our goals. The competition among lenders may still be on the main street or at the four corners of your community, but it's also in your mailbox. Borrowing is also available with Internet-based online applications and pre-approved offers delivered to you at automated bank machines. All this is in addition to "0" down and "0%" financing on big-ticket items, such as cars and major appliances. And with access to that credit, there are so many more wonderful things to do. We have clearly shifted from needs to wants. Luxury has taken over comfort as the new standard.

Along with changing family dynamics comes a growing demand for new types of homes. Not everyone wants a big house with a large garden. More and more households are made up of individuals or just two people: young couples, same-sex couples, single parents with one child. Regardless of the configuration of your household, we all seem to have higher expectations than our grandparents could have even imagined; we have come a long way from gathering around that radio in the living room or watching Ed Sullivan on the black-and-white television. Now it's the flat-screen plasma TV, or cable TV over the Internet, or Internet through the TV. With all the gadgets and gizmos out there, most of us borrow to buy what we want.

We have borrowed in a relatively random way, and now we feel stretched. Karen, our Vancouver advertising account executive, says, "I know I'm supposed to pay off those credit cards, but …" We don't get stretched by design. It is an incremental process—a student loan here, a department-store credit card there. You might, for instance, have opted for the 25-year payment plan for your mortgage, and then accepted that "pre-approved" credit card offer that came in your mailbox, which started out at 3.9% interest but is now up to 17.99%. You used that card, then got another. You didn't plan to buy such an expensive car—you just really liked it and had room on credit. We borrow to finance our aspirations, but then our values and tight cash flow get in the way of enjoying our dreams.

Era/Aspirations	Values/Attitudes	Mass Experience	Opportunities	Behaviour
1940s	"The community will help us get started"	Radio	Vendor finance from retailers	We save
1950s "more for my kids"	"I've failed if I have debt"	B&W TV	Finance companies; Sears card; Bank of Nova Scotia offered its first personal loans in 1958	We buy what we *need* when we have the means
1960s "needs vs. wants"	"I need a home"	Colour TV	Banks do mortgages and launch credit cards with Chargex (later became Visa)	We buy what we *want* when we have the means
1970s "personal freedom"	"I paid off the mortgage"	Microwave	Mortgages generally 5-year closed terms, with only monthly payment frequency	We borrow
1980s "more for me"	"I need to keep up"	BMW Pool	1986 national network of bank machines launched Banks compete for mortgage business	We spend
1990s more women in the workforce: "pragmatic" "balance"	"I've succeeded if I have a line of credit" and I use it for morally sound investments	Computers	Technology-enabled targeting "Please apply" Mass marketing of personal lines of credit	We invest
2000 "simplification and appreciation" "safe and secure"	"I've succeeded if I'm using my credit line" for comfort and luxury	Flat-screen plasma TV High-speed Internet Digital cameras	Technology-enabled pre-approvals variable-rate open mortgages	We buy more

CHAPTER 3

Consumer Concern About Debt

Now that we have a little insight into *why* we feel the way we do, let's look at *what* exactly it is that we're doing. And whether or not we should be worried about being in debt.

It's true: we are a nation of borrowers. That said, we are not a nation of clones, all operating with matched values and aspirations. Still, when it comes to borrowing, Canadians, regardless of age, geography, gender, or ethnicity, want the same things: flexibility in payment options; ability to get credit when needed; and simple, straightforward application processes with quick approval. We also want to feel confident that we've chosen the right credit product for our needs and can handle it responsibly.

Our Concern About Rising Household Debt

We all know someone, or perhaps it's yourself, for whom debt has become a burden, where the debtor is in over his or her head, or walking a tightrope, balancing between bills and paycheques. Such situations might naturally make us feel anxious about borrowing, and yet, despite such grim possibilities, we are not really worried. The November 2003 Ipsos Reid–Scotiabank Consumer Credit Poll reveals that more than three out of four Canadians say that they are comfortable with their current level of debt.

So *should* we be worried? Well, yes and no. Take a look at the two charts on the next page.

To illustrate, a $100,000 mortgage in 1990 at an interest rate of 14% required almost the same monthly payment as a mortgage of more than $200,000 today at 5%; in both cases the monthly payment would be about the same at $1,175, based on a 25-year amortization. As a direct result of low interest rates, Canadians have been able to afford more borrowing than ever.

The average household debt

Canadians' average household debt is more than $65,000, and it includes such items as mortgages, credit cards, car loans, and student loans. People with big mortgages might look at this figure and think it's too low. But don't forget, $65,000 is an *average*. When you factor in that 60% of Canadian households don't even have a mortgage and many others are very close to

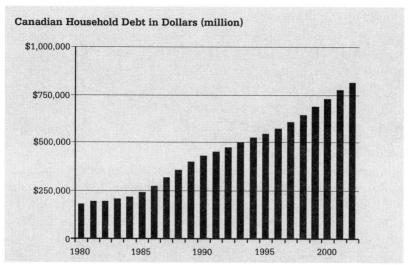

Canadian Household Debt in Dollars (million)

This chart of Canadian Household Debt shows total consumer borrowing in Canada since 1980. You can see that as the population has grown and as debt has become more affordable, we have increasingly borrowed. And our overall growth in borrowing has exceeded our growth in income.

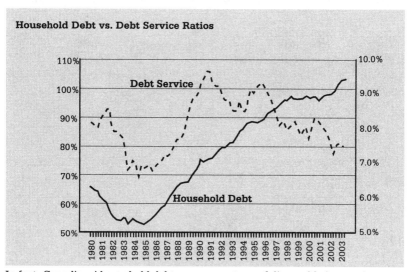

Household Debt vs. Debt Service Ratios

In fact, Canadians' household debt as a percentage of disposable income has exceeded 100%. Scary? No, not under the circumstances. Looking at this chart, you can see that even though the amount of debt we carry relative to our disposable income is higher than ever, the very low interest rates are keeping the cost of debt at low, manageable levels compared to the past twenty years.

paying off their mortgage debt entirely, $65,000 starts to seem a little high. And when you look at how it has grown over time, it starts to seem higher. Higher still when you look at the average household income. But that's the problem with averages—they don't tell us what the situation is in each household.

Attitude towards borrowing

People's attitude regarding debt varies to some extent by where they are in life and the level of debt they are carrying. Younger households, that is, households run by people younger than 35, review their debt more frequently than do older households. But then, people under 35 are more likely to have more debt to review; they carry about one-third of total consumer debt in Canada, and as more young people become homeowners, that debt is increasing. The households that are driving the growth in credit are the higher-income households, which are most likely to be able to handle it, and the increase in their borrowing is increasingly in personal lines of credit. Households headed by someone younger than 45 represent about two-thirds of total consumer debt.

Who carries all this debt?

While we expect younger households to carry debt to build their assets (home, education, car), we tend to assume that people over 65 have no debt left. That may have been the case in the past, but not anymore. The age of borrowers has shifted up as baby boomers and their parents continue to spend, enjoy items of instant gratification, and have a relatively high comfort level with borrowing. In fact, households headed by someone 55 to 64 have increased their debt load by about 14% to $43,000 in just one year. Now these consumers are paying down their borrowing, but still, households with members older than 65 are carrying an average balance of $23,000. And these are the same people who pay off their mortgages and throw parties to celebrate, while continuing to carry other unsecured, unnecessarily high-cost debt. This is clearly not the best strategy.

Is anyone debt-free?

There are households that have no debt at all. About one-quarter of Canadian households report being debt-free. A few of these just haven't started yet, but more are older and have paid all their debt off. Most people, regardless of affluence or comfort with debt, hope to be debt-free by the time they reach their early 50s. That said, the average age target for becoming debt-free tends to increase as we get older, making this a bit of a moving target and so not always reached. Relatively few among us have simply saved up for purchases.

In fact, eight out of ten Canadians agree with the statement that they are "living for today and not worrying about tomorrow." And Canadians are using credit to do that living.

Benefits of debt

Canadians are well aware of the benefits of having credit. We recognize that borrowing can enable the purchase of a home, a car, or an education. Credit can help us through surprises and emergencies. It can also help us get away on vacation. In many years of market research, consumers have shared the view that "credit" can give us confidence and freedom to access opportunities that would not likely be feasible without it, while "debt" feels like a burden and must be managed and paid down.

Good debt/bad debt

The previously discussed good debt/bad debt perception is also tied to specific ways of borrowing. While every instance of borrowing has a purpose, Canadians readily acknowledge that the purposes can be very different. A mortgage is clearly a debt, but one customer put his feelings about it this way: "My mortgage is a reflection that I'm grown up and financially responsible." Another customer referred to her mortgage as "smart debt because it's a fixed payment loan that gets smaller every year." In both cases, it's clear that mortgages are good debts. Lines of credit are also seen as good, or at least smart debts, since interest rates are generally lower than other borrowing options; a personal line of credit offers freedom and flexibility. Credit cards also have an important place, giving us day-to-day purchasing flexibility, with lots of interesting features, such as insurance protection on our purchases. But carrying a continuous (i.e., beyond one month) balance on a high-interest credit card is clearly seen as bad debt. Borrowers must choose from among all the options the right borrowing and transacting vehicles for their purposes.

Well, all that's very nice, but *should* we worry?

Should we be worried for ourselves, our neighbours, and our economy? We already told you that the situation is not scary, given the current environment (see previous Household Debt vs. Debt Service Ratios chart). The higher cost of real estate and the lower cost of mortgages, thanks to lower interest rates, has fuelled much of the borrowing boom. As well, because equity markets have been down, our savings have been diminished; so rather than liquidating investments while they're down, Canadians have been borrowing. True, our rate of borrowing has outpaced our growth in income, but the proceeds of much of our borrowing have been used on our homes. People are buying into the real estate market, buying up, building out. The renovation market has been huge. For those who are not directing funds to fixing up their home, many are using home-equity-secured loans to lower their overall cost of borrowing. So, much of the increase in borrowing has been for "good debt" purposes, building assets.

What we say and what we do are at odds

Paying down debt is the number-one financial goal of Canadians, with 77% of the adults polled saying it is very important to them. Yet while 62% say, "Being in debt scares me," just four out of ten who describe paying down debt as an important financial goal consider themselves very close to achieving that objective.

While we say we want to pay off debt, we are, in fact, carrying more debt than ever and we're saving less. There is widespread acceptance that Canadians have increased their spending and debt for the practical reason that with historically low interest rates, the cost of carrying debt is at an all-time low. But there is also a psychological reason. More Canadians are living for today, feeling more secure in their jobs. When times seem so good for so many, it creates an opportunity to take stock and consider how well positioned we are for the future. Because if we run into any problems, we don't have much room to squeak through. Half of Canadians would have difficulty paying down debt if someone in their household became unemployed. And a rising interest rate environment would be cause for concern for many.

How we deal with setbacks

More than one-quarter of Canadians have fallen behind on loan payments, which is actually down somewhat from previous years. But what *is* up is the number of Canadians, more than one-third, who have borrowed from friends or relatives in the past year to cope with their situation. And consistently greater than 10% of Canadians cope with their financial situation by "selling old possessions." We hope they're just referring to having a yard sale to clear out cast-off children's toys, outgrown clothes, and idle appliances, and are not selling great-grandmother's cabinet to an antique dealer or pawning heirloom jewellery.

In spite of our objective to pay off debt, most people have to borrow to own a home or a car. We need to borrow to deal with those unpleasant surprises that pop up with the tulips in spring after the first great rainstorm of the season: the wet basement, the leaky roof, or worse ... both. We want to get ahead, but more than ever, we want to relax and appreciate what we have. We don't want to get in over our heads in the process, but somehow that can happen so easily.

And it's not just the setbacks ...

As many as one in four Canadians say that their current household income is rarely or never sufficient to meet essential expenditures such as rent or mortgage payments, utilities, food, and clothing. More than one in ten say that they would rely on their line of credit or a loan to pay bills.

And these same people often deny that there is anything wrong. "I can handle it," they say. But when we look at the numbers, we know that as a community, we're getting stretched. If interest rates rise in the coming years, we're going to feel more than a little pinched.

So, we're going to start today, while things are good, to do a little reality check, shed the convenient ignorance, become aware and take control, so that we reduce the risk of feeling like a victim later.

CHAPTER 4

Homeownership: Borrowing vs. Investing

One customer recently referred to his mortgage payments as his "pre-authorized monthly deposit into a savings plan." When asked what he meant, he explained that he and his wife had just bought a bigger, more expensive home. When they retire, they'll sell the place, with any increase in value accumulating tax-free, and downsize to a small condominium. Thus the mortgage on the big house was an investment, a sort of forced savings plan.

That's certainly one way of looking at a home as an investment, and it's an especially effective approach for the truly undisciplined with a penchant for spending. But the strong emotional attachment many of us have to our homes makes establishing such a detached perspective difficult.

Before we explore the task of investing or borrowing using home equity, we need a bit of perspective on "homeownership." Recognizing the values that are so deeply rooted in our sense of home helps to explain why we do some of the things we do as borrowers and investors.

The Psychology of "Home" vs. "House"

Our homes are central to our lives as borrowers. And investors. Let's consider how they have come to be so pivotal in our lives, starting with the pragmatic definition of a *house*. According to the *Oxford Canadian Dictionary*, a house is "a building for human habitation." We generally think of a structure in which people live, situated on a piece of land, perhaps among other houses, a place that fulfills our basic need for shelter. Descriptions in the weekend classified ads might come to mind—"three bedroom reno, deep garden, fireplace, central air, updated kitchen ..." For anyone who has ever gone house hunting, that description can represent myriad possibilities. The house may be a detached, single-family dwelling or one of a series of connected dwellings, like a row house. Most believe that to qualify as a house, the dwelling must have its own roof. Otherwise it's called a condominium, a duplex, a co-owned or co-op apartment.

Now let's look at what a *home* is. The term has a subtle but important distinction from *house*. *Oxford's* definition of home takes "house" and personalizes it: "the place where one lives; the fixed residence of a family or household." The dictionary goes on to add, "The place of one's dwelling and nurturing, with its associations." When you think of home, do you see family gathered around the dinner table or a new puppy tearing around the garden? Do you think of the discreet markings on a wall that measure the growth of children? The scent of garlic bread heating in the oven, while an enormous pot of chili simmers during the Grey Cup? Home could mean the century-old farmhouse in the country that has sheltered several generations of the same family, or it could mean the loft in a converted warehouse in the indus-trial centre of a major city. A home is not always a house, and a house is not always a home. Perhaps British novelist Angela Carter said it best: "Home is where the heart is, and hence a moveable feast."

What house is to shelter, home is to security. It is a place where we feel safe from prying eyes and external pressures. Home is where we retreat when feeling threatened. Immediately upon the collapse of the World Trade Center towers, how many of us felt a strong urge to go home and be with family? Home is where we get hugs, from our children, our parents, our partners. It's where we speak our mother tongue and not the language of business. As one colleague described it, "Home is more than a place; it's a feeling that takes over me whenever I return after I've been away (even if I had a good time while I was away). You don't have to be alert to every move anymore, because you know by heart every turn. It's your neighbourhood, your street. The pinnacle of this whole picture is *my home*."

But home is also an expression of our identity. Beyond serving as the hub of family, we design the space and its contents to suit our needs and persona. Home is where "pride of ownership" is rooted. It is where we define ourselves, among family and friends, away from public scrutiny and judgement. That said, have you ever asked or been asked, "What will the neighbours think?!" Okay, the privacy factor only goes so far!

(Neither "house" nor "home" requires ownership as part of their defi-nitions, by the way, though ownership plays an important role.)

A little history

Trevor Watkins in *World Archaeology* (1990) reports perhaps the earliest example of humans using a house-type structure. He describes "a sequence of subterranean houses" that date to 8250–7900 BC and demonstrate "elaborate care and effort spent on their construction, maintenance and demolition/replacement." Details from the excavation of this site in northern Iraq are thought to represent the earliest evidence of humans perceiving a house as a home with significant social symbols of ownership.

Homeownership evolved through the Middle Ages as the structure of the household evolved. Witold Rybczynski observes in his 1986 book, *Home: A History of an Idea*, that it was members of the bourgeoisie—the merchants and tradesmen in medieval Europe—who lived in homes. By contrast, it was "the aristocrat who lived in a fortified castle, the cleric who lived in a monastery, the serf who lived in a hovel." The bourgeoisie lived in the "townhouse of the fourteenth century combining living and work." These were minimalist accommodations with little furniture, but practical. Rybczynski observes that the evolving condition of the family led to more development of the house. As children of these families stayed at home (rather than being sent out to work or for apprenticeship in the trades), space and privacy became new needs of the house design.

Ultimately, the departure from a feudalistic European system with highly concentrated landownership was achieved in the New World. However, the rationale for the rise of homeownership has been the subject of much intellectual debate: was it really a rise in demand for homeownership, or more a decline in the economic forces that favoured tenancy? Was it a basic human need to assert control over one's own environment, or the product of free land abundant in reasonably sized parcels in the early days of the new land? Whatever the motivation, it is not well documented and we are left to hypothesize. That said, if we look at the history of homeownership in Canada, whether two hundred years ago or just last week, immigrants came for religious and political freedom, and for the opportunity of prosperity. The democratization of landownership in North America worked as an enabler for that prosperity.

We can conclude that our homes have a range of functions, from shelter, comfort, and security for ourselves and our family. They offer an expression of our identity and freedom. Now let's look at the home as an investment.

Your Home as an Investment

When you buy your first home, you have taken that critical first step to making one of the most important investments in your life. It may not be a guaranteed investment certificate (GIC) or a mutual fund, but the bonus with this investment is that you can live in it. It is tax-efficient and can even generate a cash flow for you. Ultimately, the investment in home equity gives you options. The equity you build up in your home can be used to secure borrowing to finance other dreams at relatively low rates of interest.

Nancy and Thomas, a couple in their mid-40s, had built up over $100,000 in equity in their city home. They hoped to retire in ten years and live in the country. They contemplated buying a lakefront cottage property to eventually move into and live year-round, but were very anxious about taking on more debt. They had modest RRSPs and they wanted to pay off the mortgage on their primary residence before they retired. They shuddered at the prospect of the debt that would be required to finance the cottage dream. They considered refinancing the mortgage on their home, but calculated that the additional debt would require putting off their retirement for another five years. Strangely, they were less concerned about adjusting their time horizon for retirement than they were about having a mortgage on their home longer than planned. In a conversation with their personal banker, they were asked this question: if their home were a GIC used to secure a line of credit, would they feel differently about moving ahead with the cottage? They instantly acknowledged that would be completely different; they would feel much better if the investment were a GIC—but they had never considered their home as an investment. One of their grown children suggested that while Nancy and Thomas would need to work a few more years if they bought a cottage now, they enjoyed their work, and with a cottage, they could enjoy spending weekends there right away. So Nancy and Thomas decided to use the equity in their home to make their dream a reality sooner. They now own a lovely cottage, which they use mostly in the summer months, but plan to "winterize." They are even contemplating that they won't have to defer their retirement if they are willing to do minor renovations to their primary residence and rent out the basement—though their emotional attachment to their home may make such a move difficult. But at least the option exists.

When looking at your home as an investment, you need to take a long view. Most people don't realize the gains in value on their investment until they are well into retirement. The average homeownership tenure in Canada is increasing, especially as people have been entering the market sooner. Mobility is considerably lower among owners than renters. Is the tail wagging the dog a bit with this observation? Perhaps mobility is lower because renters tend to be younger people with more flexibility, as they have yet to establish their life preferences, whereas homeowners are more likely to establish roots in a community. So unless you are really talented at dealing with a "handyman's special," as real estate agents often call houses that need work, and flipping them for good gains, then chances are you're like most of us who want to find a home that meets our needs, and those of our children, over the long haul.

While a home may be seen as an investment insofar as it gives us shelter and security and our children an opportunity to be raised in a good neighbourhood in proximity to a good school, it is also seen as an investment from a range of perhaps slightly more objective perspectives, from people who have a keen interest in the value of your home.

Real estate agent

We're not about to discuss the role of the real estate agent in the home buying and selling process. That comes later. The focus here is the role a real estate agent has in developing the property value of your home, which translates into price—whether you're buying or selling. Since real estate commissions are a percentage of the selling price, obviously, the higher the price, the higher the commission. Real estate agents can be particularly talented at looking objectively at your home and assessing its value based on local market conditions, including area supply and demand. What contributes to home value? Well, beyond "location, location, location," you are likely to get a higher purchase offer and sell faster with a fresh coat of paint, an up-to-date kitchen and bathrooms, and a general condition of good repair. When that's not enough, there is also "fluffing," as one real estate agent laughingly referred to the process of clearing the clutter and setting up a house with new furniture, art, and flowers to optimize a first impression. Thus, real estate agents can help you get beyond your emotional attachment.

Lawyer

From a lawyer's point of view, owning a home means you have a legal stake in property, with title. Title is recorded in provincially managed land-registry offices, which track ownership and "encumbrances" on a piece of property. An encumbrance is any sort of claim on a property by any person or organization other than the owner. For example, a mortgage held on a property is an encumbrance, and the lender or mortgagee, most often a bank, will declare its interest in the property.

The "deed," which represents legal ownership, gives you control over your property. Though, even legal ownership has its limits, with constraints set out by your municipal by-laws. These constraints can include, but are not limited to, restrictions on property use, changes to buildings/fences, noise levels, and when you can put out your garbage. In spite of these confinements, there are few boundaries on your ownership within your property lines. The place is yours. Others are not allowed to trespass. The mortgagee doesn't really want to take over ownership of your home with a foreclosure process (a relatively rare occurrence), so pay your mortgage, your taxes, and your utility bills on time, and your title, your legal ownership, will let you enjoy your home unfettered.

While your lawyer can advise you on title issues and protection, in Canada, one of the options available to insure your claim on title and protect your investment is *title insurance*. This service can protect both you and your mortgage lender from title defects and problems. An up-to-date survey and title search through the provincial land-registry system should reveal any defects or problems, but since a current survey may not be available for homes in many older neighbourhoods or rural areas, title insurance may be accepted in place of a survey or a lawyer's search. The option to use title insurance is best made with your lawyer and simply involves a trade-off analysis of cost and time.

For example, in a hot real estate market, where there is no current survey available on the property and you want to make a clean, unconditional offer, title insurance is a quick solution to avoid delay in presenting an offer. A new survey can take a while and cost more than $1,000—at a time when you have enough expenses involved in moving! Title insurance is less expensive.

It is a lawyer's responsibility to ensure that you have clear title when you buy your home, that there are no claims against the property, either from unpaid taxes, utility bills, or liens placed by a builder or someone else. The lawyer needs to confirm that the person offering to sell the property actually has legal ownership to be able to sell it to you. Title insurance can keep your lawyer's bill down by providing an insurance policy against these issues, and it can even provide protection against fraud and forgery.

Title insurance can facilitate a smooth closing process and protect you and your heirs for as long as you own the property, but the decision to use title insurance needs to be made in discussion with your lawyer. If you have any concerns about the property, the history of the property usage, or confusion about property lines, you may be better off having your lawyer conduct a comprehensive search. But in most cases, you can enjoy peace of mind knowing that title insurance provides the protection you require. Most policies cover you as long as you own the property, and some policies will even cover your heirs. The premium, or amount you pay, for title insurance varies by region, by the value of your home, and by the nature of the policy. But the premium, usually payable with a one-time payment, ranges between $150 and $250.

Fraud is an increasing threat against the security of your home as an investment. It is effected through identity theft and forged documents. The concern about an accelerating trend in mortgage fraud prompted the Canadian Institute of Mortgage Brokers and Lenders (CIMBL) to prepare a White Paper on the topic in 2001, and they formed a Mortgage Fraud Task Force. While CIMBL is focused specifically on fraud, which they define as "any deceit within the mortgage life cycle," there is also fraud against homeowners who are mortgage free.

Types of mortgage fraud include misrepresentation to a lender of the property characteristics, misrepresentation of employment or employment income by the borrower, even misrepresentation about property use intentions. In these situations, it is normally the lender who becomes the victim of the fraud. However, the mortgage-free homeowner can be the victim of fraud when there is fraudulent transfer of title with a forged deed. A homeowner would have no reason to be aware of or alerted to a change on title. With the forgery effected, the "new" homeowner is then in a position to take out a mortgage on the property, default on repayment, and leave the real homeowner in a terrible position, with the "new" lender wanting to enforce their rights of foreclosure. While the courts have protected legitimate homeowners, the protracted settling of cases causes much anxiety.

A solution is title insurance. Just as you take out an insurance policy against property damage or loss due to theft or fire, a title insurance policy can protect you against fraud.

You can also take preventative actions: shred all mail, whether bills or other correspondence, that can be lifted from your garbage or recycling box early in the morning by someone walking along the sidewalk; if you have a mortgage, deal with a reputable lender, as they are more likely to use highly sophisticated modelling tools for fraud detection.

Banker

For many Canadians, reaching the decision to buy or rent a home is not straightforward. Each option has its advantages, depending on where you are in life. If you rent, you are not tied to one place. It's much easier to pull up stakes and move. Generally, you are not responsible for the costs associated with maintaining a rental home, and you don't have to worry about property tax and the other costs that come with homeownership. But as you know now, owning a home not only ensures more security and lends a sense of pride, it can have considerable advantages as an investment.

Bankers have often been heard saying that renting is "just a home you're borrowing from someone else." You get to use that house or apartment, but it's never really *yours*, and you avoid adding to or fixing up the place much since you can't take the built-in book shelves or new kitchen with you. But many Canadians continue to rent because they believe that they can't afford to buy. That's where Karen, our Vancouver account executive, is. But in today's market, with more affordable housing and lower interest rates, the gap between the cost associated with renting or buying a home may be closer than you think. Take a look at the following chart to see the potential difference between renting and the carrying cost of a mortgage, depending on the size of your down payment:

Renting vs. Buying

If your monthly rent is:	you can afford a mortgage (at 6%, with a 25-year amortization) of:	which, with a 25% down payment, means a home valued approximately at:
$ 500	$ 78,000	$104,000
$ 700	$109,000	$145,000
$1,000	$156,000	$208,000
$1,500	$234,000	$312,000
$2,000	$313,000	$417,000

However, there is much more to consider than just how rent payments compare with mortgage payments. That is simply the starting point to assess affordability. The model to assess the economic trade-off of renting versus owning is much more complex; it needs to take into account all the costs of homeownership—property taxes, maintenance costs, utility bills—and assess these costs against the opportunity to invest your cash and generate a return on the investment. That said, all that cash laid out over the years in support of homeownership has to be weighed against the tax-free growth in value of the equity in your home as real estate values rise, not to mention the personal satisfaction and security that comes with homeownership. No matter how many different ways we run the numbers through different models, in almost every single scenario, you will be financially better off after 25 years of home-ownership, compared to 25 years of renting.

There are only a few situations that favour renting over homeownership. They involve either very high interest rates and declining real estate values, or low rents, usually in a rent-controlled environment, and surging real estate prices. And, of course, if you're planning to move frequently, then renting is a preferred alternative. Ultimately, though, if you're looking at the long term, you can be confident that homeownership is a better investment than renting.

Even if you think you'll just break even on your investment in a home versus investment in the equity markets, one of the most compelling aspects of homeownership is the knowledge that every monthly mortgage payment you make brings you closer to owning the home outright, at which point monthly payments stop. Rent never stops, and it always increases. So home-ownership starts to seem even more attractive when you consider what your level of income will be in retirement years.

From the perspective of your banker, another way to look at your home as an investment is that your mortgage can be put in your RRSP. Yes, a mort-gage is a loan, but it can also be converted into an investment with the assis-tance of an investment broker. In this process, you put your mortgage into a self-directed RRSP. In effect, you then pay your mortgage interest to yourself. Sounds good, right? It can be. But this option is not available to everyone. First, you need enough contribution room in your RRSP to be able to load in the entire balance of your mortgage. Second, every self-directed RRSP has fees associated with this arrangement, including mortgage insurance premiums and often a one-time mortgage set-up fee. As you can see, this is not an entirely straightforward transaction, so to determine if this option could work for you, you need to discuss it with your investment advisor.

Accountant

An accountant may be able to help you optimize the value of your home, depending on how you use your residence, and the potential tax implications. The primary tax advantage of homeownership is the tax-free capital gains you can generate when it comes time to sell your primary residence. But you may be able to create some tax efficiency in the meantime if you have a home-based business or home office. And there may be other opportunities to create tax advantages. You should also understand the tax implications if you have rental income from your home. But since the rules can change, you'd best discuss your own tax situation with a tax accountant, who will be an expert on the subject and up-to-date on the rules.

Economist

Economists study the role of housing in the economy, which contributes to consumer spending and employment. Think of all the different people employed in your community who earn a living based on growth in housing. There are developers, architects, and builders. There are several tradesmen, including plumbers, electricians, brick layers, and carpenters. In your munic-ipal offices, there are planners. And then consider all those people involved in maintenance, not to mention the furniture manufacturers, designers, and decorators. Housing helps keep our economy humming, and to the extent that we have a healthy economy, you can generally anticipate growth in the value of your home!

Community leaders

A range of studies across numerous countries, conducted over several years, consistently reveal that homeowners have a higher turnout on election day than do renters. These same studies show that homeowners are also more likely to be community activists. But while homeownership bears a strong correlation with community participation, we'll hypothesize that renters are as likely as homeowners to be concerned about top items on the political agenda (health care, education, taxes, crime). Still, public policy at both the federal and provincial levels favours homeownership, with tax incentives and opportunities to use RRSP savings without penalty for down payments. As well, rent-control policies encourage developers to build condos rather than apartments. It is a widely held belief that homeownership is good for society as a stabilizing force in the economy; this conventional wisdom is good for your investment.

Taking Advantage of Home Equity

Your equity in your home grows in two ways: first, as you pay down the mortgage; second, as your property increases in value. But to realize the tax-free equity growth of your principal residence, you need to sell, not always an attractive option. Your home can also be a source of incoming cash without your having to liquidate the investment. Perhaps the most obvious example is the rental opportunity that arises when a big event takes place in your city, creating demand for accommodation, and you can rent out rooms, or even go on vacation to avoid the crowds and rent out your whole house. No doubt many Vancouver residents will take advantage of this opportunity during the winter Olympics destined for that city in 2010.

There are also more ongoing opportunities. A colleague of ours has dreamed of taking months away from the city to sail around the world. He anticipates strong demand for his city centre loft as a rental property. He'll feel more comfortable leaving the place in the hands of a responsible tenant than leaving it empty. And his adventures can be financed, at least in part, with the rental income. Sure, you say, but that's an interesting downtown loft and I live in a rural area—who's going to want to rent that while I head off to warmer climes in the winter? Well, perhaps a young family whose members love to ski and are willing to pay several thousand dollars each winter for a weekend escape destination. One of our customers is a widow with an elegant and gracious original stone farmhouse just north of the quaint community of Creemore, Ontario, and another with a great, still-red, old schoolhouse with bell intact. They are completely different residences: one is on major acreage, the other stands on a single acre; the first is enormous with plenty of bedrooms for the teenagers, while the other is just one big room offering a dorm-like experience. Both homes are primary residences, which are rented for the winter while their owners use the income to help finance their warmer winter residences.

You must understand the risks and legally protect yourself if you rent, so that you can take action if tenants don't pay or don't move out when they said they would. Get a rental agreement in writing.

You don't necessarily have to vacate your home to generate rental income. The bed-and-breakfast business is booming. Whether you're in a known tourist destination or even a less obvious place, the B&B option can be interesting. A retired colleague has opened her lakeside home as a B&B in a small fishing community, where travellers are treated to warm hospitality while they relax over breakfast on the patio surrounded by a beautiful garden. The income generated from this small business is intended to cover the rising property tax, so that retirement savings aren't depleted. In Ottawa, we know a lovely couple whose children are grown, leaving them with a large, but empty home. So they take in regular business travellers from Toronto and Montreal. It offers great company to the homeowners, some steady income, and a very affordable and comfortable solution for the business travellers. While operating a bed-and-breakfast may involve a fair bit of work, you can generate some welcome income if you manage your budget carefully.

If having someone else live among your possessions feels a bit daunting, but you need the income, there are other options. A *reverse mortgage* is one way to get cash from the equity you have built up in your home. While reverse mortgages have not yet been widely adopted in Canada, they are widely available in the US and the UK from a number of providers. At home, we have the Canadian Home Income Plan (CHIP), which was established in 1986 and which offers reverse mortgages through most major banks.

What is a reverse mortgage? It is a loan against your home that requires no repayment while you live in the house. You draw between 10% to 40% of the value of your house, with the specific amount depending on your age and the property value. Eligibility requires that you own your home and are at least 62, and that you draw only up to a maximum of $500,000. Subject to meeting the criteria, you draw funds to generate cash for yourself. Then, you use the cash however you like: invest it in an income-generating vehicle or even give the cash to family members so they benefit from the value of your estate while you're here to enjoy it with them. Or you can use the cash just to pay the bills. That can be helpful with big bills like property tax or in-home health care assistance. It's entirely up to you.

But why, you may ask, draw equity out of your home instead of withdrawing extra funds from your RRIF (assuming you had an RRSP and set up an RRIF, or registered retirement income fund)? Well, what you take out in a reverse mortgage is tax-free and is not treated by CCRA as income that would affect other government benefits that seniors may receive, whereas withdrawals from a RRIF are taxed at your marginal tax rate. You may be better off leaving your investments inside the RRIF to grow tax-free and draw as little as possible to minimize your tax bill. Ultimately, the funds you draw out of your home equity with a reverse mortgage are paid back if and when you sell the house, or by your estate.

There must be reasons *not* to use a reverse mortgage, you protest. Well, do you have an image of being put out of your home by the "lender" if home values were ever to drop? You can ease some concerns dealing with CHIP because they commit that ownership remains in your name and you can never be asked to move or sell to repay. And CHIP commits that the loan amount to be repaid "is guaranteed not to exceed the fair market value of the home at the time it is sold." So if you take out a reverse mortgage, the balance of the contents of your estate will be protected for your heirs. You do need to keep the property in good repair, pay your property taxes, and maintain fire insurance. Interest does accumulate and compounds every six months, so you or your estate could have a sizable interest bill. But with today's low interest rates, the service is more compelling, and you do have the option to pay interest annually so that there is no interest obligation in the end, only the principal repayment. And if you choose to pay the interest one year, you don't have to pay it the next—the program is relatively flexible that way. Gordon Pape, one of Canada's most knowledgeable and popular financial writers, has endorsed CHIP's reverse mortgage, saying he is "impressed by the value of the Canadian Home Income Plan Reverse Mortgage as a wealth management tool for seniors who want to stay in their home." It certainly is an option that makes sense in some situations for retired people who need extra (and tax-efficient) income. Like any financial solutions, you're best advised to discuss with your banker a range of options that may meet your unique needs.

Another option for later in life is the obvious one: downsizing. Moving to a smaller home. This is often the most difficult decision to make. It's not easy to leave the home where you've lived for years and raised your family, where you know every bulb in the garden, where the bus schedule is as familiar as your face in the mirror. Still, a retirement community is attractive to lots of people who like the company of people their age, where there are fewer stairs to navigate, and generally less maintenance to be done, which translates into lower costs. You may also save on property taxes.

But we're skipping ahead here. If you're just starting out on your home-ownership journey or if you're still early in the process, then you need to focus on how to pay off the mortgage to really optimize your home value as an investment. (More on the best way to pay off your mortgage in Chapters 7 and 8.)

People ask us all the time, "Is it a better investment to buy in the city or the suburbs?" "Should I be looking at a residential neighbourhood or downtown property?" "Where will the demand be so that I can make the best investment: big house or small house or condo?" At the end of the day, it really comes back to your needs. How do you want to live your life? If you have children, or plan to, where do you want to raise them? What trade-offs are you willing to make—a large house in the suburbs with a nice big yard and a long commute, or a smaller house with virtually no yard but a very short commute? Don't try to second-guess the housing market. A house must first and foremost be a place that you want to live in and make yours; it must meet your lifestyle needs.

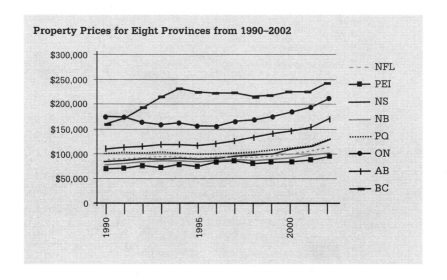

Property Prices for Eight Provinces from 1990–2002

Any seasoned investor in the stock market will tell you about the challenges of market timing; you can't second-guess the stock market. You simply need to invest, stay invested, and continue to invest regularly. If you look at any market index's performance over a five-year period (that's more than 1,200 trading days), the 10 or 20 best market days of that period can represent enormous gains—but no one can ever predict accurately when those days will occur. Similarly with homeownership—no one can predict when real estate values are going to spike or even out. But we all recognize that real estate has generally been a solid, stable investment over the long haul. So focus on what's important for you over the long term.

And we really must dispel any remnant of the overly simplistic notion that "a house is a poor investment." Whoever tries to sell you that story is usually using market-timing examples of the 1989 real estate crunch or the impending doom of suburbia. Whether your motivations are pride of ownership, security for yourself and family, or forced savings paid to yourself (rather than a landlord), investing in a home is unquestionably a sensible thing to do!

CHAPTER 5

What's on the Horizon?

Don't we all wish we had a crystal ball? It probably wouldn't do to look *too* far into the future, though. Things are happening so fast, we might miss something! But taking a look at where we've been and what we've been doing lately as Canadians, we can at least contemplate what the near future holds for homeowners.

The post-war move to suburban bliss in the 1950s and 1960s has set many of the benchmarks for our expectations in the early twenty-first century: spacious, detached single-family dwellings with lush green lawns, mature trees, and friendly playground parks in close proximity. These post-war years saw a tremendous rise in the birthrate—the baby boom—and these ideal neighbourhood homes were inhabited by large families, with stay-at-home mothers who began enjoying some freedom from the tedium of housekeeping with the help of home appliances. But perhaps the most significant social and economic change in the latter half of the twentieth century was the growing participation of women in the workforce. Additional income made detached single-family dwellings a financially viable goal for lots of people.

Now layer increasing numbers of immigrants onto that scene. New immigrants generally moved into major urban centres, where rental properties met their needs until they were ready to buy their own home. In a recent study conducted by the CMHC, based on 1996 census data, immigrants who have spent more than 20 years in Canada have a higher rate of home ownership, 77%, compared with those of us born in Canada, 65% of whom own our own homes. And now, households headed by immigrants who are well established in Canada are more likely to occupy single detached houses—62%, compared with 58% for non-immigrants. Other sources show that the higher rate of immigrant ownership is a function of the higher rate of immigrant households being made up of families, while non-immigrant households, by comparison, have a higher rate of individual occupants.

Demand for new styles of simplified, highly convenience-oriented housing (like condominiums) has taken strong hold. Plus, younger buyers are the highest growth segment of the home buying market. In fact, *almost half of homebuyers in Canada are under 35 years of age,* and 48% of the home buying market is made up of individuals or households of two people. While there may be demand for small, condominium style housing, CMHC reports in their *2003 Major Market Highlights Study of Consumer Intentions* that about 11% of Canadian households planned to buy a home in 2003. Among these households, a "large majority with two or more people plan to buy a single detached home: 68% of two-person households, 75% of three-person households, and 82% of households with four or more people." With relatively high levels of immigration anticipated to offset declines in natural population growth, evolving definitions in family, and greater ease of individual housing, demand is expected to remain high across a range of housing styles and neighbourhood types.

Home Developments

Regardless of whether your interest is in an urban loft or a suburban four-bedroom home with a big yard or a place in the countryside, developments in home styles span every type of neighbourhood—and many of these developments are driven by technology. Our busy lives need vehicles of convenience, and so home has come to be a place where clever electrical and electronic appliances reign supreme. Dr. Sheryl Hamilton, an assistant professor in the Department of Art History and Communication Studies at McGill University in Montreal, published a paper in the *Canadian Home Economics Journal* in the spring of 2003 that highlights this perspective, examining the "home of tomorrow."

In her paper, Dr. Hamilton addresses the evolving role of electrical appliances in our homes and how they have, and have not, changed our roles: women are still primarily responsible for management of the household. Dr. Hamilton looks at how we have imagined new appliances over the last fifty years. Some of these are quite entertaining, such as F. Ross Jr.'s forecast in 1958 of a "laundro-matic unit that will wash and dry clothes even as these hang in the closet." Wouldn't we all like one of those! The paper also points out how far we've come: it wasn't until the 1960s that major appliances like washing machines and dryers became commonplace in our kitchens and laundry rooms; microwave ovens didn't start appearing till the 1970s. While we haven't yet quite achieved that all-in-one appliance, amazingly, in the September 2003 edition of *House and Home* magazine, there was a brief review of dual-purpose appliances featuring an all-in-one washer and dryer from LG. "The Direct Drive washer/dryer combo automatically starts to dry once the wash cycle is finished." It goes on to say that it requires "no special venting and plugs into a standard 120-volt outlet." But even better for some is the all-in-one oven, dinner warmer, and refrigerator. "Whirlpool's

Polara oven is also a fridge that keeps food fresh for up to 24 hours before you're ready to cook it. Program the cook time and the unit starts supper for you. Running late? It keeps your meal warm until you arrive. Missed dinner time altogether? After two hours' warmth, it refrigerates that meal." If that's not enough, there are lots of other nifty appliances, most of which are loaded with computer chips to make them "smart." Now that's progress!

But advances go beyond appliances. It's incredible how far we've come with construction materials and building processes over recent decades, which have freed us from tasks like waxing floors. While our homes are not completely wired for networks to interconnect all our computers and digital-capable appliances, we soon may be able to skip that re-wiring process altogether. Think "wireless." If we can connect to the Internet on computers the size of our palm, which also work as a telephone, why would anyone have to make holes in their walls to rewire?

Our home styles will evolve as the way we use our homes changes. We've started to see signs of this with more open space, whether it's a loft or a "great room" or a multi-purpose kitchen. We can imagine children more likely doing their homework on the computer in a high-traffic zone like the kitchen or adjacent family room, rather than upstairs at a desk in their bedroom, as parents tackle the challenge of on-line chatting or games during homework time, and as concern about on-line safety of children persists. We see older children staying at home longer and older parents who need care moving in with us. All of these developments will have an impact on home uses and floor plans.

We may not ever have the Star Trek Replicator, but we have come some distance from the Flintstones. What we ultimately get is greater and greater ease of housekeeping, which frees us to spend more time with our families, at the cottage, enjoying personal interests, or if you must, at work. And, homeownership will be made easier for individuals and small households. We'll see more mixing of home types as urban planners try to integrate different styles of housing into communities. And our cities will continue to grow.

With this growth and the strong demand across a range of home styles, you can be optimistic that your investment in your home will hold its value. Reasonable estimates put an expected increase in the average resale home value at just under 5% in 2004. Not a bad rate of return when you consider that it's tax-free. Of course there are local and regional variations, for location really does matter. Vancouver, Calgary, and Toronto have had very strong growth in real estate values, and based on most indicators, Montreal remains the most affordable of our large cities.

Housing Affordability

Housing affordability is primarily a function of three variables: house prices, interest rates, and taxes. House prices across Canada have increased by an average of 25% over the past 10 years, but that increase has not been at a steady rate, in that national house prices increased in value by 9.5% in 2002 alone. National averages, however, can conceal actual affordability in specific communities where home buying activity may be more frenzied. So let's be more precise: over ten years (1992 to 2002), average house prices increased by about 23% in Vancouver, 53% in Calgary, 28% in Toronto, 39% in Ottawa, and 27% in Montreal. But these figures obscure the real rise in housing prices in urban communities where there has been considerable growth in condominiums. While condominiums can represent premium property ownership costs depending upon location, size, and amenities, the growth in smaller units over recent years has diffused the average growth in real estate values in many urban markets.

If we look at the average home value as a ratio of household income, then affordability has clearly diminished with the rising level of house prices and more modest increases in personal income. However, a closer examination of real affordability requires an integrated view of house prices, interest rates, taxes, and cost of utilities. Even in this more comprehensive view, there has been some diminishment in affordability, but low interest rates have offset much of the surge in housing prices that we've seen in most regions of the country.

If you are looking for the bubble on real estate values to burst, planning to hold off your real estate purchase until prices come down, don't. While there has been a frenzy of reports in the media of houses that have skyrocketed in value, take a closer look at the details of each situation, such as how much money the homeowner invested in renovations over the past five years to upgrade the kitchen, bathroom, wiring, and garden. Now, did the house really double in value? From the purchase price ten years ago? Perhaps. But from the total investment? No.

So why will real estate hold its value? In our opinion, it comes down to four basic factors:

1. *The cost to carry a large mortgage is low by historical standards*
   With higher home values come bigger mortgages. This is sustainable as long as interest rates continue to float at relatively low levels and mortgage payments on larger homes are more manageable by more people. In this context, real incomes don't have to rise at the same pace to support increasing home values.

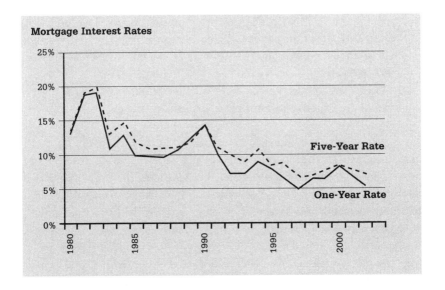

Mortgage Interest Rates

2. *The cost to rebuild supports today's prices*
You need to consider what it would cost to replace the house. With material and labour costs increasing, particularly in a strong renovation market, housing prices don't seem so inflated. Since we don't foresee double-digit mortgage rates on the horizon or underemployed contractors, the cost to rebuild is unlikely to tumble.

3. *Demand is strong versus supply*
Demand has remained strong as more people shift from being renters to homeowners. This situation is different from the late 1980s when there was an enormous supply of new housing and much of the demand was fuelled by investors (more than homeowners) who were "prospecting" in real estate and "flipping" properties. Speculative demand petered out, reducing property values, and leaving homeowners with mortgages higher than their home value. Today, the supply-versus-demand situation is on a more even keel. Yes, supply versus demand is location-sensitive, but the balance is still widespread, with demand distribution outweighing supply in most markets.

4. *The real growth rate is sustainable*
Any asset that grows in value at less than 10% a year is not growing at a booming rate; again, it's not a bubble ready to burst. To be more precise, home values have grown at an average rate of less than 5% a year in

Canada from 1959 to 2002. In the US, home prices have increased every year in that same time period, with an average growth rate of 4.8%. The highest annual growth rate in real estate values in Canada was 9.5% in 2002, with all provinces having had gains in home prices.

So we don't anticipate that current values will do anything but stabilize in some regions and continue to increase in others.

In fact, with baby boomers well established in their urban homes, many are turning to rural properties for weekend retreats. Ski chalets, country homes, hobby farms, and cottages are all experiencing increasing demand as recreational properties. But not only are boomers contributing to this increasing demand, a lot of retirees are giving up their city homes and moving to the country. They can trade in their city dwelling for a reasonable return, find spacious accommodation in the country, which they can manage mortgage-free, and so free up some cash to finance their retirement, while generally paying lower property taxes. So, don't expect any great real estate bargains outside the city limits, either, particularly in high-demand areas.

Of course, there is always the unexpected. We can't promise that the value of your home will increase steadily for years to come. It is likely that your real estate will hold its value based on the four reasons we have set out above, but if there is a drop in value, what does that mean for you? Well, it could mean lower property taxes if you are in a market-value-assessment area. It could also mean less cash in your pocket if you were planning to sell your home sooner than later. But if you have taken the long view and you continue to make your payments, then nothing changes. And eventually your property value will be restored.

While the housing market is expected to remain strong with demand outpacing supply (as affordability remains within reach), an environment of somewhat increasing interest rates is taking shape. While no one is expecting interest rates to rise at a startling rate, nonetheless, as they rise and home-equity increases begin to stabilize, we can expect reduced mobility. Enthusiasm for trading up and refinancing will dampen, which will reduce supply and soften demand. As well, we should expect more pre-payments against mortgages and other borrowing as interest rates shift upwards.

There's an element of concern in the air about what lies ahead if interest rates rise. Everyone needs to seriously assess his or her own risk tolerance here. If you are locking into a mortgage for five years, what is your risk threshold expected to be at the other end of the term if rates have increased? Will your income have increased enough to cope with higher payments, or do you think you will be able to pay down the mortgage to a level to keep payments at a manageable level? We're not contemplating a future of doom and gloom with interest rates peaking at more than 20% (as they did in 1981) and plunging real estate values. It is conceivable, however, that rates could increase by 50%. If your mortgage is currently at 5%, then 7.5% is within the realm of possibility. What does this mean for you? Well, on a $10,000 one-year term mortgage (with a 25-year amortization), at a rate of 10%, a rate increase of 25 basis points, or .25% means an increase of only $1.69 in your monthly payment. Consider some bigger numbers: on a $50,000 five-year term mortgage, at a rate of 10%, an increase of 1% means an increase of $34.02 a month. And if your mortgage is $75,000 with an amortization of 15 years, at a rate of 5%, an increase of 2.5% in rates means a monthly increase of almost $100. So you'd have to have a really big mortgage and rates would need to rise a lot for most people to be put into an unmanageable situation. If you *are* feeling vulnerable, a brief conversation with your banker can help you with this cost-sensitivity analysis.

> Let's look at **Maria and John** again, and what an interest rate increase would mean for them.
>
> Maria and John bought their new house for $185,000 and they had a down payment of $15,000. So their mortgage was for $175,525 (including their mortgage-default-insurance premium of 3.25%), which they locked into a five-year term with a 25-year amortization at 5.55%, with payments every two weeks of $538.25. They are now one year into the term. It's possible that interest rates could rise a percentage point or more in the next four years. What would that do to John and Maria's payments?
>
> When their mortgage matures in four years, based on the balance still owing at the time, it would take an increase of only 2.60% to add about $200 to the amount of their payments each month.

Flexibility in Borrowing Options

Not only are there developments on the horizon for your home style and affordability, but there is also continual development in the borrowing options lenders provide. Let's consider a few of the key developments that are emerging in Canadian financial services, particularly as they relate to financing a home.

Easier access to homeownership

First, we expect to see a reduction in the barriers to entry into homeownership, as requirements for borrowers are lowered. In particular, we expect to see even smaller down payments required on home purchases. Look for a "no down payment" option. While many people find that with low interest rates, the cost of carrying a mortgage and paying property taxes and utility bills is within reach, just coming up with the money for a down payment can be a real struggle. By easing the down payment requirements, more people can make the move from being renters to owning their homes. The insurance premium you'll pay for this sort of option will be higher, so you need to assess the trade-off of paying more now, but enjoying homeownership sooner.

Advances on pricing

As a general rule of thumb, the pricing on your mortgage, if you opt for a fixed rate, will be driven by such considerations as term and size of the mortgage. Generally, larger mortgages in longer terms (for example, a five-year term, as opposed to a one-year) may qualify for better pricing. By contrast, variable rate mortgages, which have been priced at a discount to the prime rate, have been popular lately, in a low prime rate environment.

Another important development is the reduction of opportunities to haggle with your lender about the interest rate on your mortgage. More and more lenders are introducing low, non-negotiable rates, especially on longer terms. Pricing is becoming more dynamic and model-driven, allowing lenders to offer better rates to more people. Lenders differentiate themselves through price offers, which can include Scotiabank's Cashback (to cover acquisition and appraisal fees), discounts from posted rates, or unique products. The increasing advances in automation will help to drive down costs of borrowing and improve service.

Also on pricing, we expect to see a shift towards more performance-based pricing. This is a relatively new approach to pricing, introduced recently on credit cards and lines of credit and is, essentially, the better your credit risk, the more regular your payments, the less you'll pay. If you miss payments, your rate will go up to compensate your lender for the risk. We anticipate seeing more of this type of pricing, and it could be applied to mortgages one day to ensure that the best customers with the strongest relationships and best credit performance are able to get the best rate.

Bundled solutions

In an effort to help customers simplify their banking needs, we expect to see more bundled solutions that integrate a range of service into a single, comprehensive program. About ten years ago, banks in Australia launched all-in-one deposit and borrowing accounts. The National Australia Bank calls their service a FlexiPlus Mortgage, and they describe it as an all-in-one facility that combines a customer's everyday transaction account, mortgage, savings, and investments. While some people appreciate having just one account that shifts from being a big borrowing facility to savings and investments, Canadians generally prefer to compartmentalize and have their savings accumulate separately.

The most comprehensive borrowing solution in Canada today is one offered by Scotiabank, called the Scotia Total Equity Plan. We're asking that you indulge our plug for our STEP program. But it really is a unique borrowing solution. In fact, this program has been featured globally as a market-leading solution, so we're very proud of STEP and the customer satisfaction it fuels. What exactly is STEP? It's a borrowing package that lets you bundle all your borrowing, including your mortgage, line of credit, VISA card, personal loans, and overdraft protection into one program; you can even have different mortgage accounts or lines of credit set up for different purposes. Unlike other all-in-one accounts we've seen in Canada, STEP includes only your borrowing: you keep your deposit and savings accounts separate. The benefit of this plan is that it secures your borrowing with the equity built up in your home (or in your cottage or a rental property you own), so that you can take advantage of lower interest rates. You then use the savings in borrowing costs any way you want: to pay off your mortgage faster, catch up on your RRSP contributions, pay off higher-rate credit card balances, or pay for your children's education. STEP provides a more affordable way to achieve your financial goals, with a comprehensive, consolidated statement. STEP is the ultimate revolving credit facility for life.

We expect to see more and more people using revolving credit (rather than term loans), as we adjust to having credit throughout our lives, and flinch at the thought of having to reapply for borrowing again and again. So the objective is to have one credit limit established with one application and create a revolving credit plan that we can access whenever we need (or want). The shift to revolving credit reflects our preference for simplicity, with flexibility, and credit available to us over our lifetime.

We also anticipate longer amortizations becoming available for homeowners. The standard 25-year amortization of a mortgage reflects our objective to pay off our borrowing, but it has also historically reflected the "useful life of the property" as assessed by lenders. But we know that our houses are well built, and we are injecting a lot of money into home repair and upgrades, making the useful life of the home, by most standards, much more than 25 years. As interest rates start to rise, the option to extend amortizations over a longer period will help younger people keep their payments low and affordable. Then as their incomes rise, they can increase their payment size and reduce their amortization. The longer amortization also reflects the preference to have revolving credit for life, secured by home equity. We're not there yet, but can imagine that someday soon, people may have the option of setting up their borrowing for longer time frames.

Access to services

Canadians are relatively high users of electronic banking services. On a per capita basis, we are reportedly, of any country in the world, the highest users of high-speed Internet services at home. We have more ABM (Automated Bank Machine) usage and functionality, and even more advanced Internet banking. This puts more power in the hands of consumers to manage their financial services with greater access points and convenience. While we are all familiar with the ability to make deposits, withdrawals, and balance inquiries at a bank machine, there has also been quite a bit of development on electronic banking for borrowers—if your mortgage is with a bank, you may be able to check your balance at an automated bank machine or through on-line banking on the Internet. Some banks even offer comprehensive, up-to-the-day statements for customers who bank on-line. And mortgage pre-approval applications are available over most banks' web sites.

The Internet is likely to shift over time from being a research facility to offering greater transaction and advice capability, as broadband technology enables more personal interaction. In an article in the *McKinsey Quarterly* (2001, No. 2), McKinsey consultants reviewing financial services in Europe point out that "many customers who were unwilling to use services over narrow-band dial-up connections felt more comfortable with the idea of broadband services because they are easy to use, fast, and secure." They go on to say that mortgages are an area of service where currently consumers have a relatively high need for advice and low level of acceptance for on-line interaction. Consumers participating in the McKinsey study "consistently said that they wouldn't buy a mortgage without face-to-face human contact." It appears, then, that we still have some distance to go.

Yet given young people's higher levels of acceptance of Internet transactions and the more experienced, knowledgeable position of people moving into their second or third home (who have renewed mortgages several times), we can anticipate greater developments in on-line capability and Canadians' acceptance rates of it, especially around borrowing applications and refinancing.

Without the benefit of a crystal ball, predictions for the future can only be projections based on what has happened in the past. We know there will be technologies we haven't even dreamed of yet, which will advance the financial solutions available to you. There could be new competitors in the marketplace as globalization of financial services evolves. In the end, all the new services and service providers are likely to provide their customers with increasingly greater benefits in choice and flexibility.

CHAPTER 6

Where Do I Start?

D id you always think that Dorothy in the *Wizard of Oz* was the first one to say, "There's no place like home! There's no place like home!"? Well, actually, Dorothy was quoting J. Howard Payne, the early-nineteenth-century American actor, poet, and playwright who penned "Home, Sweet Home," which was first performed in Covent Garden, in London, England, in 1823 as part of the opera *Clari, the Maid of Milan.*

> *'Mid pleasures and palaces though we may roam,*
> *Be it ever so humble, there's no place like home;*
> *A charm from the skies seems to hallow us there,*
> *Which sought through the world is ne'er met with elsewhere.*
>
> *An exile from home splendour dazzles in vain,*
> *Oh give me my lowly thatched cottage again;*
> *The birds singing gayly, that came at my call,*
> *Give me them, and that peace of mind dearer than all.*
> Home, Sweet Home
> J. HOWARD PAYNE (1792–1852)

Homeownership Basics

Buying a home is an exciting event, and for most of us, the single, largest financial transaction we will ever complete. You should buy if you like the idea of being a homeowner and have the financial resources to do so. You're better off *not* buying a home if you don't like to stay in one place, or your job doesn't allow you to stay in one place, or you don't want the responsibilities of homeownership and the maintenance required.

If you already own a home, why move? There are lots of reasons:

- You have a long commute to work, and you want to lessen that and create more family time.
- Your current home needs significant upgrades and you don't want to tackle them, or you don't think the place is worth the investment.

- You have changing space needs, such as a growing family.
- You need to be closer to aging parents.
- You're getting older and don't have the energy to cut the grass or shovel the snow anymore.
- You're tired of your 60-year-old house and prefer the more spacious design of a new house.
- You're sick of the noise and pollution in the city and want to live where it's quieter and the air is cleaner.
- Your children have grown and left home, and now your place seems too big.
- Your neighbourhood has been transformed again into a place for young families, and you want neighbours at the same stage of life as you.

If you're trying to decide *when* you should buy your first home, or move to a larger home, or downsize, you simply do it when you're ready. It takes a bit of homework to prepare yourself, some math to calculate what you can afford, but more emotional commitment than anything. And let's repeat: it is not about market timing, but rather when you are ready.

Finally there is *how?* You need to do three things:

1. *Decide what is important to you in a home.* Do you care if your home is a detached single-family dwelling or a row house? What about a shared driveway or a shared garage? We have provided some examples to help you here whether you are new to the process of home buying or if you've been through this a few times.

2. *Decide what you can afford.* There are a few aspects to this. And again, we have laid out examples and tables to make it easy for you to calculate. (They follow the tables of the three households.)

3. *Get organized for your house hunting.* Look at homes that may be of interest and be prepared to make an offer when you find what you want.

What is important to you in a home?

Then think about location. Where do you want to be in the community? Consider the amenities you want to have nearby. Is traffic an issue between where you will live and where you need to get to—work, doctor, grocery shopping? What about noise-makers like trains, planes, and automobiles? Ultimately, you need to consider what surrounds your home in terms of the things that could add value or detract from your investment. By creating a list

Karen

On her own and expects to be that way for a while, but likes to have nieces and nephews for sleepovers and likes to have space for TV, reading, and computer that is separate from living/entertaining area.

Loves to garden, but really has little time.

✓ prefers condo with balcony for container garden

✓ wants view of the water: bay or ocean

✓ wants to be near city centre for ease of access to work and friends

✓ needs two bedrooms and will use one as a multi-purpose study, TV room, guest room

✓ needs one bathroom, but prefers one en-suite and one powder room

✓ wants big windows to capture the sun

✓ prefers a condo building with long track record of good management with reasonable monthly maintenance fees

Conclusion: with interest rates low and free down payment mortgage option available, Karen has set out on her hunt for a small condo

Maria and John

They have made their move and are staying put for a while. They have found that the house they bought really meets all their needs—they were very clear on what they needed and wanted, so when they set out on their search for a home, they were prepared to move quickly on an offer when they found the place that worked for them.

✓ need family community

✓ need big yard with lots of grass

✓ need to be close to parents

✓ want quick access to highways for John to get to work

✓ want nearby amenities, including shopping, so Maria's outings with the children aren't complete torture

✓ need four bedrooms (have five)

✓ need two bathrooms (have three) with a powder room on the main floor

✓ wanted a main floor family room and a large kitchen (have both)

Conclusion: staying put for a while with room to grow

Alya and Sandor

Children may be grown and are out on their own, but it's amazing how often someone shows up looking for a comforting space.

Need room for the Ottawa grandchildren sleepovers, and concentrated family appearances on the holidays.

Alya would be happy with a garden service and can afford it. Sandor loves to experiment with different colours, but doesn't enjoy the tedium of deadheading daisy bushes.

✓ want a house with more space than their old row house, and with less repair work

✓ want bigger rooms

✓ want a small yard which could be container garden with planting area on the perimeter

✓ want minimum two bedrooms plus a study or three bedrooms

✓ want minimum two bathrooms

✓ want a place in good repair. Haven't the time or skill to cope with a fix-up special

Conclusion: real estate values in Montreal for a nice spacious home are within reach with a modest mortgage, so plan to move up with your priorities, you can focus more quickly on what you need, and what you want.

Keep in mind the real estate adage "location, location, location!" You may find a great house, but if the location isn't right, the house won't seem so great anymore. Whereas, if the "bones" of a house are good and you're in a location you love, you can upgrade to make the structure more comfortable.

Consider our three households, who are getting or have got their checklists up to snuff. Then take a stab at your own, using the table in Appendix A.

Decide what you can afford

There are essentially four things you need to look at to determine if you can afford the sort of house you want:

1. the down payment
2. closing costs
3. the size of payments you can afford
4. carrying costs on the house

What you can afford reflects a combination of these four variables.

The down payment

Coming up with 25% or even 5% of the purchase price as a down payment can be a real challenge. Let's look at ways that may help, or at least help you consider the trade-off between getting your home now while mortgage rates are low, and waiting and probably paying more for your home, with a mortgage at a potentially higher interest rate.

Even if you've managed to save a little, sometimes it isn't enough to cover closing costs, moving, renovations, and all the other unexpected costs that could catch you by surprise. If you are ready to buy now and your cash flow can support ongoing payments, you may not have to wait to buy your home. The Scotia Free Down Payment Mortgage is an affordable fixed-rate mortgage designed to give first-time home buyers the money they need to get into the housing market. It's available as an affordable five- or seven-year insured, fixed-rate mortgage that provides the 5% minimum down payment as a gift. While there is an insurance premium required, as is the case with any high-loan-to-value-ratio mortgage (which we discuss in more detail in the next chapter), you can get into the home you want before interest rates and real estate values rise, putting that home out of your reach. To get information about down payments, check your lender's web site.

If you don't meet the minimum requirements for a free-down-payment mortgage, there are other options that may be available. For example, if you're buying your first home, you and your spouse may each be able to withdraw up to $20,000 tax-free from your RRSP to use as your down payment. The Canada Customs and Revenue Agency (CCRA) gives you up to 15 years to pay the money back into your RRSP, in annual instalments. (It is important to get the "loan" from your RRSP repaid on time; otherwise you'll be obliged to pay tax on that amount.) The only requirement is that you haven't owned and lived in a home as your principal residence in the five calendar years prior to the withdrawal. For more information on the RRSP Home Buyer's plan, visit the CCRA's web site at **www.ccra-adrc.gc.ca**. Or your personal banker can help you determine if the RRSP Home Buyer's Plan is right for you.

Another way to get started, if you have a bit of time on your side, are the homebuyer savings plans offered by some banks, which may be ideal. Here's how the Home Bonus Savings Plan works at Scotiabank: when you set up a monthly savings plan of $200 or more each month, the money you save will be regularly invested in a high-yield savings account that provides a solid and safe return. For each savings year completed, you'll be entitled to receive a bonus when you use your down-payment savings towards a new Scotiabank mortgage. The matching gift tops out at a maximum of $1,000, in effect creating an even higher return on your savings. It's an easy way to earn more money to put toward a down payment for your new home.

Cashback is another great feature to look for from your lender. You may qualify for a percentage of your new mortgage back in cash, which you can use however you choose. Let's face it, old milk crates as chairs in your new home aren't very glamorous or comfortable. If you need to buy furniture, light fixtures, appliances, or window coverings for your new home, the bills can really add up. So Cashback can be a big help at a time when expenses are running high.

Whatever it takes to get started, there are solutions available from lenders to get you into a homeownership position sooner than you think. Talk to your lender about the options that may be available to you.

Closing costs

When you're looking at a house, you need to think about more than the price as you consider your costs. There are also the infamous "closing costs." Let's look at what these might include and where you can get more information to ensure that you're well prepared.

Perhaps the most significant closing cost is a provincial or munipical tax. It is paid by you, as the purchaser. In Ontario, Manitoba, and Nova Scotia, it's called the "land transfer tax." In BC it's the "property purchase tax." Ironically, in Quebec, it's called the "welcome tax." Regardless of what it's called, it's always calculated based on the property value, and it can be a complicated calculation. This is one of the more misunderstood and overlooked expenses

Ontario Land Transfer Tax and Quebec Welcome Tax on a property of $260,000
= ($55,000 x .5%) + ($195,000 x 1%) + ($10,000 x 1.5%)
= $275 + $1,950 + $150
= $2,375

BC Property Purchase Tax on a property of $260,000
= ($200,000 x 1%) + ($60,000 x 2%)
= $2,000 + $1,200
= $3,200

Manitoba Land Transfer Tax on a property of $260,000
= ($30,000 x 0) + ($60,000 x .5%) + (60,000 x 1%) + (50,000 x 1.5%) + (60,000 x 2.0%)
= 0 + $300 + $600 + $750 + $1,200
= $2,850

by first-time home buyers. Your real estate agent should be able to give you an idea of what the tax might be, depending on the price range you're looking at. But forewarned is forearmed, so ask well in advance or do a query on your realtor's web site to see if they have a quick calculator tool, to get a sense of how much you might have to pay. If you're buying a new house, then you may not have to pay the land transfer tax, but you will have to pay the GST, which may or may not be imbedded in the price of the house.

In addition to the taxes, there are adjustment costs, which are expenses that need to be settled between the purchaser and the seller upon closing, such as municipal property taxes and utility bills. If you're moving into the house in the middle of a billing cycle, the utility will need to split the bill between you and the previous owner.

Then there are legal fees and/or title insurance. You can anticipate at least a $500 bill from a lawyer, depending on the complexity of the legal work involved in your purchase transaction and whether or not you purchase title insurance, which can range from $150 to about $250, depending on the coverage you're looking for.

If that's not enough, there are a few other expenses to keep in mind when you buy a house, which may or may not be applied:

- Home inspection cost on an existing house. Expect to pay a few hundred dollars for a comprehensive inspection. While you are not required by law to have an inspection, it's a good policy. Many purchasers will present an offer that is conditional on the home passing an inspection. Other prospective buyers, engaged in a hot bidding war, may choose to bypass the condition. Even if you don't make the passing of a home inspection a condition on your offer to purchase, it's still a good idea to have one done if your offer has been accepted, so that you know at the outset what some of your immediate and longer-term home-repair costs will be. That way you can budget accordingly, before you go out shopping for furniture or committing to expensive decorating projects.

- Survey fee on an existing house. Expect to pay $700 to $1,500 depending on the complexity of the property line. Some homeowners do not have a survey available on the property. You may choose to have a survey completed to ensure you know exactly what you're buying—the property lines and any rights of access.

- Appraisal fees. The cost of having an independent, objective appraisal completed on the property you're purchasing is about $200 for most urban properties. The cost can be higher in rural communities or if there is complexity with the home and property.

- Mortgage registration fees. This is the cost charged by the province to register your title and mortgage on the property you're acquiring. While the fee will be paid by your lawyer, you need to anticipate that about $120 to $200 will be included in your lawyer's bill to cover this expense.

- Moving expenses. These will depend entirely on how much stuff you have, how far you're moving, and whether you use a well-known moving company, an independent business, or your family and friends, in which case there is still the price of a case of beer and pizza!

- Don't overlook the service-connection fees applied by utilities. Some even require a deposit against future services. When our friend Jim moved recently, Toronto Hydro wanted either a $200 deposit or bill payments set up with pre-authorized payments. He opted for the $200 deposit, but if your cash flow is tight, the direct-payment option might be best. You can get your deposit back after three years if you have demonstrated that you pay your bills on time—but you have to ask for it.

- If you are selling your home be sure to factor the real estate agent's fees into your transaction costs. These fees normally run up to about 5% of the selling price.

- Finally, you may want to plan for a decorating expenditure to update your new home if it seems a little tired. That might require new curtains, a coat of paint, or some fresh flooring. Even a new set of handles or knobs on kitchen cupboards can perk up that room. And new light fixtures can make a big difference. Or maybe it's a new piece of furniture or two. Even some gardening work may be needed. Whatever the condition of the house and depending on your priorities, it's always nice to have prepared for some expense so that you can make this house into your home.

If you *budget about 3% of your purchase price for closing costs*, you will generally be safe if you're buying an existing house, but that's before you consider anything for decorating. With a new home you'll need to plan for more because of the GST (unless it is included in the purchase price), and to cover more extensive decorating to complete the house (like curtains and light fixtures).

What size payments can you afford?

How big is the ongoing monthly mortgage payment going to be? The size of your mortgage payment is really a function of the size of your mortgage and prevailing interest rates. You can then make adjustments based on the frequency of your payments and the amortization you choose. Think of the amortization factor along a scale with a trade-off between lower payments today and higher amounts of interest paid over the life of your mortgage: the faster you pay off your mortgage, the higher your payments will be. The longer you stretch out the amortization, the smaller your payments will be— and as a result, the more house you can afford. Yes, in the long run, you'll be paying more for your house, but if this is the only way you can afford the home you want, then go for it!

Here is a schedule of monthly mortgage payments using different interest rates and amortizations, but all based on a mortgage principal amount of $100,000, so you can see how far your money might stretch.

Mortgage payment table over various rates and amortizations

Interest Rate	25 years	20 years	15 years	10 years
4.00%	526.02	604.25	738.04	1,010.89
5.00%	581.60	657.13	788.12	1,058.15
6.00%	639.81	712.19	839.88	1,106.51
7.00%	700.42	769.31	893.25	1,155.94
8.00%	763.21	828.36	948.15	1,206.41
10.00%	894.49	951.66	1,062.27	1,310.34
12.00%	1,031.90	1,080.97	1,181.61	1,418.03

Above is just a look at selected mortgage payment amounts. If you want to be more precise, you can log on to your bank's web site, where you'll probably find a mortgage payment calculator. Try **www.scotiabank.com** and input some different scenarios into our *How Much Will My Mortgage Payments Be?* calculator. You can get a pretty good gauge of what you can afford before you even talk to a lender.

It is not unusual for a lender to approve you for a bigger mortgage than you can really afford. This is not a ploy to get you in over your head; it's just that the lender can't know or, for that matter, judge your personal lifestyle choices. Many items in your monthly expenses, such as your habit of going out to a movie every week, are of no interest to your lender, who is only interested in your *fixed* expenses. These are all the non-negotiables, including your rent or mortgage payments, utility bills, loan payments, spousal and child support, and taxes. Bottom line, you're the only one who knows what you can really afford. So *you* need to factor in the monthly expenses that your bank doesn't look at.

What if your bank approves you for less than you think you can afford? Shop around. But keep in mind that most lenders use similar decision models. Lenders recognize that using more than about 32% of your household income on housing costs (called Gross Debt Service Ratio, see Glossary) can stretch you to a point where you can get into trouble. And no one wants you to be in a difficult position where you can't afford your payments. The more information you share with your lender, the better equipped they are to help you find a solution that meets your needs and situation.

Carrying costs on the house

If you have been renting, it is very easy to miscalculate what your ongoing expenses might be when you buy a house. If you have been renting a place within walking distance of your work, but then move to a house a bit farther away, you'll need to add the cost of transportation to your regular expenses. If you've been renting, then you may never have seen a utility bill or property tax bill—and can they ever add up. Develop a Monthly Expense Review to track where your money goes now (Appendix B). It helps to run a pro forma column of predicted costs with homeownership so that you can mitigate the surprises. And there will be lots of ongoing expenses in addition to the one-off projects: removing old broadloom, or painting the bathroom, for example. The roof will need replacement in about three years, and what about those eavestroughs? How much do you expect to spend each spring on your garden? Whether you budget for condominium maintenance fees or the on-going upkeep of a house, you need to include something in your plan.

The same surprises can pop up if you move from a new house to an old house or from the city to the country. For example, you will have no water bill in the country if you draw from a well. You'll have costs to maintain your well and water-pump system, but there is no regular water bill from a municipal water utility.

Similarly, if you move from a relatively new house to a much older house, you may find there is more structural maintenance work, depending upon the quality of materials that were used in your new home. Still, replacing the mechanical systems (plumbing and wiring) in an old house is no small undertaking.

Get organized for your house hunting

To start, you need to get your ducks lined up. Who do you need to be involved in your home-search-purchase transaction and what are their roles?

Real estate agent

Whether or not you use a real estate agent to help you look is up to you. But the Canadian Real Estate Association lays out some of the benefits and explains that the role of a Realtor is to "make the transfer of property as easy as possible."

One of the most successful ways to find a Realtor with whom you'll be comfortable is getting a reference from family or friends who know someone familiar with the neighbourhood you're interested in. You can also scout the real estate section of the local paper to see who has the listings in the area and even meet with a few agents before making your choice. Your Realtor should know the condition of the local housing market and be able to advise you on your approach to presenting an offer and guide you through the process. Before you commit to using a particular Realtor, either as a seller or purchaser, make sure your expectations are clear—and it's best to set out the terms of the relationship at the outset. This way, there is no confusion in what can be a highly complex and emotionally charged life event.

Lender

Unless you have a lot of cash, you'll need a lender who will give you a mortgage. The early part of this chapter and Chapter 7 explain everything you should know about mortgages, but for now let's focus on how you get your financing lined up to be able to make an offer. All the other decisions about your mortgage can happen after that.

Start with the pre-approval advantage, while you're starting to look at houses. With a pre-approval, you get two things: you can confidently look at houses in a price range that you know is within your reach, and you get the lender's commitment to a specified mortgage interest rate. That rate commitment lasts for a fixed period of time, usually from 60 to 90 days. Some banks may extend the rate guarantee for up to 120 days. With a pre-approval, your lender approves the amount of your mortgage and gives you a written confirmation or certificate specifying the rate commitment.

For people entering the housing market, you may find it has become an increasingly competitive environment, depending on the local market conditions. You may feel pressed to submit an "unconditional" purchase offer if you find you're in a bidding-war situation. But it is important to understand that

The term Realtor is a trademark identifying real estate licensees in Canada who are members of the Canadian Real Estate Association (CREA). REALTORs adhere to a strict Code of Ethics and Standards of Business Practice. The code of ethics is a firm set of rules, describing what kind of performance you have a right to expect from a REALTOR. It's your guarantee of professional conduct and the best in service.

A REALTOR's commitment to high standards of professional conduct works to the advantage of buyers and sellers alike.

A REALTOR is knowledgeable about developments and trends in real estate. A REALTOR will get you the facts: comparable prices, neighbourhood trends, housing market conditions, and more.

A REALTOR is committed to on-going education to increase competence and effectiveness in real estate trading.

Every REALTOR has been trained and tested. Their strict code of ethics ensures fairness to all parties in a transaction.

REALTORs pledge to be honest in disclosing property information and forthright in providing the facts needed to help you make one of the most important decisions of your life.

And remember, only a REALTOR, a member of The Canadian Real Estate Association, has access to the Multiple Listing Service®, Canada's most powerful real estate marketing system.

That's why many buyers and sellers turn to a REALTOR. As a member of their local real estate board, a REALTOR has his finger on the pulse of the housing market. You can trust a REALTOR to protect your interests and to look after details. And all the while, you're an active partner in the process, working with a REALTOR, every step of the way.

wherever possible, offers should be made conditional upon financing. While a pre-approval gives you a lot, it is not the final approval on the mortgage; you still need a final approval subject to an appraisal of the value of the home you are buying. If you submit an "unconditional" offer that is accepted, and the appraisal does not support the purchase price, then you could find yourself

Pre-approval Form

Karen has applied for a pre-approval. Here is what it looks like:
* Required information

Personal Information

Ms.*		Karen				Smith	
Title		First name		Initial		Last Name	

(604)	555	1212		karen.smith@abc.com
Home Phone Number *				Email Address[1]

Date of Birth *

1972		March		6
Year		Month		Day

SIN

Single		English
Marital Status		Language of correspondence *

Current Address:

10		Main		
Street #		Street Name *		Unit #

Vancouver		British Columbia		V6V 6V6
City *		Province/Territory *		Postal code *

Rent		Residential Status *

8		Years

Time at this address *

Yes

Do you currently deal with Scotiabank? *

If yes, please provide your ScotiaCard Number

Not Applicable

Employment and Income Information

Current Employment

Employed

Occupation Status *

Marketing

Occupation *

ABC Advertising

Employer Name *

Marketing

(604)	555	5555

Employer Phone Number

Ext:

Your Business Phone Number

5		Years		0 Months

Length of Employment

$5000

Gross Monthly Income*

forfeiting your deposit (usually 5–10% of the purchase price, paid up front when the offer is submitted). While a pre-approval is not a final, iron-clad approval on the mortgage, it can still help you avoid the disappointment of finding a perfect home and then not being able to come up with adequate financing.

You can apply for a pre-approval at most financial institutions by stopping in at your local branch or by visiting your bank's web site. Many of these web sites provide on-line calculators that will give you an idea of the kind of mortgage for which you may qualify. These calculators come up with an estimate based on the three C's of lending: Capacity, Character, and Collateral. These principles apply regardless of the type of credit you're considering, whether it's for a credit card, a line of credit, a car loan, or a mortgage. Before you apply for a mortgage, or even a pre-approval, you should know your monthly expenses. Be as prepared as possible.

Should you use a bank, a mortgage broker, or a finance company to get your mortgage?

Mortgage brokers are not usually lenders. They identify your mortgage needs, specifically the amount of money you need, and the term you're looking at, and then they connect you with a lender, like a bank. A broker may offer a convenient way to shop around for different types of mortgages. Brokers are paid a fee by the lender for generating the business (you don't normally pay the broker). However, it is important to be aware that brokers will direct your business only to lenders with whom they have an established relationship. They don't necessarily deal with every lender, so you may risk missing out on products that may be of interest to you if those services are offered by a lender that isn't on your broker's list.

A finance company offers the advantage of approving loans even where your credit history may be a bit shaky. Just keep in mind you'll probably pay a premium rate.

Then there are the banks, credit unions, and *caisse populaires*, which are interested in your business and should make a real effort to help you get the mortgage that meets your needs. Most banks even have mortgage specialists who can offer solid advice on this very significant transaction, along with providing a complete range of financial services beyond the mortgage.

Lawyer

Your lawyer will represent your interests as you present your offer and will be required to work through the details required for closing. The lawyer works through the transfer of title and title defect issues, and manages settlement on various disbursements. On closing day, you can expect your lawyer to hand you the keys to your new home, which have been received from the vendor's lawyer when the latter has cash in hand (your deposit plus the funds advanced from your lender, which creates the mortgage).

Appraiser and home inspector

We have already talked about appraisals and inspections as part of the costs you should expect on closing. Banks typically require appraisals prior to funding an approved mortgage to ensure that the property value is in keeping with the value of similar properties in your area. Your lender can do an appraisal the traditional way with a full tour through the home. In some cases, a "drive-by" will suffice; if the home is included in a database of real estate assessments, then an "automated" appraisal may meet your lender's needs.

A comprehensive home inspection should provide a detailed assessment of the following items: roof and eavestroughs; exterior facing; structural components and insulation; electrical, heating, cooling, and plumbing systems; interior components such as condition of walls, ceilings, windows, doors, and basement or crawlspace. The report you receive should detail the condition of the components and any work needed, with an estimate of costs for repair. Keep in mind that a home inspector doesn't have x-ray vision and can't see what's behind the walls and under the floors. He may also not be able to climb up on the roof in the middle of winter. So there are limits to the counsel they can offer. And there are no credentials required to become a home inspector, so look for a reputable firm that has a long track record to be sure you're getting a reliable, experienced perspective.

The inspection report is different from an appraisal. The inspection should give you a bigger-picture perspective of not only the structural characteristics, but also the quality of your home. It should identify structural deficiencies or problems like the presence of asbestos insulation or out-of-date wiring. A home inspection will tell you what you'll need to fix, and approximately how much it might cost. By contrast, the appraisal will provide your lender with an objective opinion on the value of the home in relation to local market conditions.

If you made the inspection a condition on your offer to purchase, you may find that you're in a good position to use that report in your negotiation to urge the vendor to effect some of the repairs that are needed prior to closing, so that the costs sits with them. At least, you'll be better informed. For all these reasons, an inspection is a way to protect the most important purchase you're likely to ever make.

Property insurer

A property insurer will cover the value of your home and contents in the event of fire or other forms of damage. If you have a mortgage, your lender will require basic property insurance covering the replacement value of your house to be in place as a condition of advancing funds on the closing date. Property insurance costs will vary depending on the value of your home and the deductible you choose on the policy, and whether or not you have a home security system. A higher deductible means the insurer won't be paying out on smaller claims, so they can reduce the overall cost of the insurance to you. But read your policy carefully to understand what it covers and what it doesn't cover, so you have no surprises down the road if your pipes freeze and burst, or lightning strikes.

When you have found the home you want, you may need to jump through a few hoops to get it. This is especially the case if real estate agents are talking about a "sellers' market." In this situation you are looking at a limited supply of houses relative to strong demand from buyers. It's not uncommon to see houses selling at or above asking price, and bidding wars become relatively routine. But even if you feel as if you have paid a premium for your home because of a bidding war, remember it's clearly a desirable investment in the view of others. And keep in mind this is also your shelter, so instead of paying rent to a landlord, you'll be building tax-free equity in your own home.

> **Tip:** Establish the price in your mind that you'd be willing to pay—and the price at which you'd be heartbroken if you learned the house went for that amount and you missed it.

Now that you've made it this far, you may be wondering how you will manage to keep all this top of mind as you work through the process of looking for a house. There's help with a quick reference summary in Appendix C.

CHAPTER 7

What You Need to Know About Mortgages

A good 80% of Canadians say that a mortgage is their most important financial decision. In fact, 82% say that their home is their most important investment. Yet it's remarkable how little we actually know about mortgages, how they work, and the hidden costs. Everyone simply defaults to cocktail bragging rights on the interest rate they scored in negotiation with their lender, only to find that rates have dropped in the ensuing months or someone else got a better rate. In the end, it's not really about who got the lowest rate; it's about who got the mortgage that best meets their needs.

Canadians believe that applying for a mortgage is a relatively complex process, compared to, say, opening a chequing account. There is a lot on the line. And with low interest rates having drawn an increasing number of younger households into the housing market, people have been looking for advice. They turn to family and friends, and they turn to the Internet. But most people looking for a mortgage are inclined to engage in a personal discussion with a banker. Here is what you need to know about mortgages, to help you prepare.

Origins of the Mortgage

Let's start at the very beginning. What exactly *is* a mortgage? Back to the *Oxford Dictionary*: "The conveyance of real or personal property by a debtor to a creditor as security for a money debt, with the proviso that the property shall be reconveyed upon payment to the mortgagee of the sum secured within a certain period." Gosh, that's clear, isn't it?

Our lawyer says that the contract or obligation was originally called a "dead pledge" (*mort* means "dead" in French) and it goes back a very, very long way in law. At the time, when you received funds with a mortgage, you literally assigned your property to that person who was advancing the funds to you. So, in effect, the property became theirs until the mortgage was paid off. When the debt was paid, the ownership was conveyed back to you. But in the meantime, your property essentially became the property of the mortgagee, and you were at their mercy (and hoping for a benevolent lender).

William Shakespeare is often cited for his reference to being mortgaged in the introduction to one of his sonnets to a Dark Lady, written in the late 1590s. That sonnet captures the early essence of the meaning of "mortgage" in that the sentiment is one of being at the mercy of another's will, which can be destructive and merciless. In Shakespeare's "Sonnet 134," there are many metaphors with legal and financial terms, which were not particularly flattering, since in Shakespeare's time, dealings with money-lenders were considered rather foul transactions conducted in shadowy alleyways. While Canadians may love to hate their banks, we do ascribe a higher level of integrity and stewardship today to these institutions. In that same sonnet, Shakespeare likens love to a tormenting and repugnant, power-based transaction with a money-lender. It is so disheartening that even with repayment of the debt, the borrower is still not freed.

Shakespeare Sonnet 134 (the boldface is ours):
So now I have confessed that he is thine,
And I myself am mortgaged to thy will,
Myself I'll forfeit, so that other mine
Thou wilt restore to be my comfort still:
But thou wilt not, nor he will not be free,
For thou art covetous, and he is kind;
He learned but surety-like to write for me,
Under that bond that him as fast doth bind.
The statute of thy beauty thou wilt take,
Thou usurer, that put'st forth all to use,
And sue a friend came debtor for my sake;
So him I lose through my unkind abuse.
   Him have I lost; thou hast both him and me;
   He pays the whole, and yet am I not free.

And Now …

Much has changed since that very early definition of a mortgage. The view now is that while the mortgage represents a charge, or claim, against the property, you, not the mortgagee (lender), still own your property. And the only point at which the mortgagee really has any rights against the property is if you default on your payments. So let's look a little more closely at mortgages today by covering some basic definitions:

A *conventional mortgage* is a loan secured by real estate on which the loan amount is less than or equal to 75% of the value of the property. So if the property value is $175,000, then the maximum amount of borrowing under a conventional mortgage would be $131,250 and you would need a down payment of at least $43,750.

A *high-ratio mortgage* or *insured* mortgage is a loan secured by real estate on which the borrowed amount is greater than 75% of the value of the property, up to a 95% maximum. You still have to come up with a 5% down payment. The federal Bank Act requires that high-ratio mortgages be insured by a third party (either the public insurer, the Canada Mortgage and Housing Corporation—CMHC—or a private insurer like Genworth Financial, formerly GE Mortgage Insurance), to protect the lender against possible borrower default, which gives lenders the ability to offer mortgages at the lowest possible rates. This mortgage loan insurance pays the lender the balance owing on the mortgage in the event of default. To arrange for a high-ratio, insured mortgage, the borrower pays a one-time insurance premium, which is calculated as a percentage of the borrowed amount.

Premiums in August 2003

Loan-to-value ratio	Purchase Premium on Loan
Up to and including 80%	1.00%
Up to and including 85%	1.75%
Up to and including 90%	2.00%
Up to and including 95%	3.25%

Mortgage insurance premium

Karen wants to buy a small condominium that costs $190,000. She hasn't saved enough for a down payment. But she can qualify for a mortgage with a gifted down payment (provided by her lender), as long as she pays the mortgage insurance premium of 3.4% for this offer. Here's how that works:

Karen's gross monthly income (before all deductions like taxes) is $5,000, which is her annual income of $60,000 (including her base income of $50,000 and the normal $10,000 bonus), divided by 12. Based on her income, the maximum mortgage for which Karen may qualify is $204,310. This qualification assumes the following:

Property Taxes $167

Monthly Heating Costs $50

Monthly Condo Fees $200

Term and Interest Rate 3-Year Closed Fixed rate of 5.8%

Amortization 25 years

Karen's mortgage insurance premium will be 3.4%, or $6,137, which will be added to her mortgage. So her total mortgage will be $180,500 (95% of the price of the condominium) plus $6,137 for a total of $186,637, and she has been pre-approved for a mortgage of more than $200,000. So she knows she can afford to make an offer on the condo she has found.

For **Maria and John**, who have a high-ratio, insured mortgage but who had an 8% down payment, let's look at how their premium was calculated and how much they paid:

The purchase price of their house was $185,000, less their down payment of $15,000, which leaves a balance owing of $170,000. Because they borrowed 92% of the value of the property, their mortgage default insurance premium was 3.25%. This worked out to $5,525, which was added to their mortgage principal. So the total mortgage was setup for $175,525.

A visit to your bank or to the CMHC or Genworth Financial web site can tell you what the current premium rates are for an insured mortgage.

How is a mortgage different from a line of credit or a loan?

A personal line of credit offers a set credit limit against which you can draw funds as needed with a cheque or through your bank's automated banking systems (including bank machines, telephone banking, and Internet banking). Lines are set up on a secured or unsecured basis. When borrowing is "secured," it means that you have pledged collateral; if you are unable to make your loan payments, the lender can use the "security" to recover their loss. Eligible security can include GICs, government bonds, or T-bills, and select Money Market funds, in addition to real estate. When real estate is the security, then a secured line is usually set up as a second mortgage, and so is a charge on your property behind your regular mortgage account. The interest rate on a line of credit is generally tied to prime, and rates are lower for higher-credit quality customers and those who secure the line with real estate. Repayment is generally set at a modest two or three percent of principal, though many lines may require only interest payments each month (subject to a modest minimum). And you can fully repay or fully redraw to your limit at any time. So, unlike an amortizing, fixed repayment mortgage loan, a line of credit can continue to be drawn from, as long as your credit is in good standing, and can be paid off at your convenience without interest penalties.

A personal loan combines some of the features of both a line of credit and a mortgage. A loan can be secured or unsecured. Like a line of credit, a loan is fully "open" and can be repaid at any time without penalty, whereas, like a mortgage, a loan generally has a fixed payment, term, and amortization plan, and your interest rate may be fixed or variable, floating with the prime rate. Amortization periods range from five to 25 years, depending on the purpose of the loan. For example, a loan secured by a car or motor home may have a maximum amortization of five years (depending on the size of the loan and the age of the vehicle), while a loan secured by real estate may be amortized over 25 years. The extent of the amortization is often defined by the useful life of the underlying security. So a car loan may have a relatively short amortization if the value of the vehicle is expected to diminish rapidly. Personal loans are generally priced higher than a mortgage because they offer the flexibility of totally open repayment at any time without penalty.

So, now that we understand what a mortgage is (and isn't), how does it actually work? Every mortgage is made up of a combination of features and payment options, with varying degrees of flexibility. The amount borrowed is called the principal, and interest is added to the principal, which compensates the lender for use of their funds and the risk they take, even if it's nominal—Canadians are extremely diligent in making mortgage payments.

Mortgage payment frequency

Mortgages are set up with a regular repayment plan, which can mean that payments are made every week or every month, or bi-weekly (every two weeks) or semi-monthly (twice a month). Where do you start? First consider how often and when you receive your own income. It is usually preferable to line up mortgage payments with the frequency of your payroll. Then, consider that the more payments you make in a year, the faster you will pay off the mortgage and the less interest you will pay. So by making payments every week or every two weeks, instead of once a month, you will actually have paid down more at the end of each year in a relatively painless way.

> **Tip:** Accelerate the frequency of your mortgage payments. Weekly or bi-weekly payments can save you thousands of dollars and cut years off the life of your mortgage.

Maria and John set up bi-weekly mortgage payments. By doing this, they will make two extra weeks' worth of payments each year—26 payments over twelve months—reducing their amortization by almost four years and saving more than twenty thousand dollars compared with a monthly payment program, based on their current interest rate of 5.55%. Of course, if their rate were higher, they would save even more.

A few other important definitions

Let's look at a few key terms we have used and should clearly understand.

Amortization is the number of years it will take to repay your mortgage in full. This is often set up as 25 years when the mortgage is first arranged. The amortization you choose will affect the size of your payments. If you want to pay off your mortgage in less time and save paying interest in the process, the amortization will be reduced, but you'll need to make bigger payments. Or if you need a little flexibility with cash flow and want to keep your payments smaller, then you can optimize the full 25-year period.

The *term* is a much shorter period, usually between six months and five years, though seven- and ten-year terms and even longer are available. The term is the period in which the contract between you and your lender is set, with specific interest rates and payment amounts. At the end of each term, you generally renew your mortgage, selecting a new term. With interest rates at such low levels, and five-year mortgage-term interest rates available at close to or the same as short-term interest rates, most Canadians taking out new mortgages or renewing have more recently opted for longer terms, like five years. Regardless of where rates have been over the past decades, the majority of borrowers in Canada, particularly first-time homeowners, have selected longer (five-year) terms. We favour the payment predictability, which provides more comfort around cash flow. Renewers tend to choose shorter terms.

> **Tip:** Select the maximum payment amount you can afford. Even a few dollars extra per payment can result in significant long-term savings.

What is a *yield curve* and why should I be interested?

A *yield curve* is the line on a graph that economists plot to chart interest rates (on bonds) over terms between three months and about thirty years. In a "normal" yield curve environment, shorter-term interest rates are lower than longer-term rates, reflecting the lower risk in the near term. The longer-term is full of unknowns, and investors need to be compensated more for committing their funds to an investment for the long term. Normal yield curves have prevailed as the average interest rate structure over the past thirty or more years.

An "inverted" yield curve is where short-term rates are higher than long-term rates. And, a "flat" yield curve means that rates are the same for both short- and long-term rates.

Yield curves, however, are subject to some interesting aberrations. We have experienced "inverted" yield curves at different times in our history, including

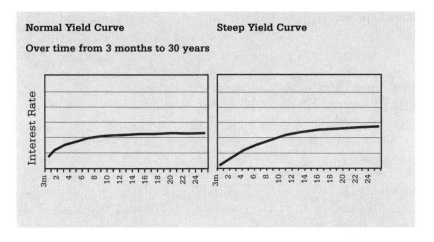

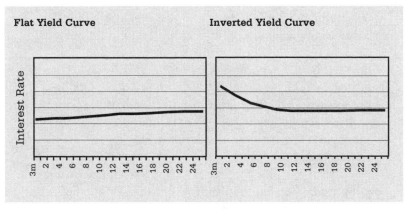

the early 1980s (perhaps most acutely in the summer of 1981), but these situations are relatively rare. The only time longer-term investors might accept lower interest rates than short-term investors would be when there is an expectation that rates are likely to drop. And they have to drop a lot. If you reflect back to the early 80s, interest rates were at an all-time high and were not considered sustainable—chequing accounts were paying over 17% interest and mortgage holders were paying over 20% on their borrowing. The prime rate was over 21%. This was just not sustainable, so short-term money was very expensive. And longer-term investors were prepared to accept less for their investments, because within a few years rates were expected to be much lower than prevailing levels, and that would put them ahead for the long term.

Steep yield curves prevailed in the early to mid-1990s, as we emerged from a recession. To create a steep yield curve, there needs to be a more acute distinction between short-term and long-term rates, compared with a normal yield curve. We see steep yield curves emerge when the economy looks as if it is on the brink of expansion. In this case, longer-term investors want a better return in anticipation of growth in the economy and rising inflation. Flat yield curves, like those we saw at the dawn of the new millennium in January 2000, indicate for the economy that there is no greater risk locking in your investments over the longer term, compared with the short term.

Understanding the yield curve is important because it can have a pretty strong bearing on what you pay in interest over the life of your mortgage. You don't need to be an economist to understand this simple model and to use the information of yield curves to guide you in the selection of your mortgage term. This is the essential point: given the normal sloping yield curve, you will pay a lower-interest rate for a short term (six months or a year) and a higher rate on longer terms (three years and more).

Okay, you say, if that's the case, why would anyone lock in for a long term? There are two reasons:

- When there is the combination of (1) a flat yield curve and (2) a relatively low-interest-rate environment. With this combination, locking in longer means you're not paying any more than you would on a short-term mortgage, but you're getting the benefit of commitment to a low rate for a longer period. This is particularly attractive in a situation where interest rates are expected to rise.
- Go long when your risk tolerance of a rising interest-rate environment is low. If you are a first-time homebuyer and have really stretched to buy the best house you can afford, then you may not be able to cope easily if your payments go up by even a moderate amount. Whereas if you commit for five years, rates may drop, or they may go up, but at least you are confident that you can meet your payment obligations. By the time the mortgage comes up for renewal, hopefully you will have had some increase in your income, and all the expenses involved in a new house will be behind you. So if rates have risen, you're in a better position to cope with bigger payments.

Research shows that most homeowners have an advantage if they routinely renew their mortgage into shorter terms. And historically, the average prime rate has been lower than the average five-year fixed rate by more than 1%. But this doesn't necessarily lead to the conclusion that a prime-based variable-rate mortgage will always be better than a regular fixed-rate mortgage. While the variable rate will probably remain below the level of a five-year fixed rate in the future, it could increase above the level of the five-year fixed rate that you can obtain today. It is virtually impossible to predict the level of interest rates five years from now. Your personal profile, including risk tolerance (how much risk does it take to keep you awake at night?) and cash flow, will determine what works best for you.

You need to weigh your goals and plans and risk tolerance in selecting the term and type of mortgage that's right for you. If you're planning to move sooner than later, you may want to take out a shorter term. Though if you can get a great rate and your mortgage is "portable," then you may be able to take that great rate with you for the balance of the term to your new home.

Fixed rates vs. variable rates: what's the difference?

We can't wrap up the discussion on interest rates without considering the difference between fixed rates and variable rates. A fixed-rate mortgage offers you the security of knowing exactly what your rate and payment will be. This is a great option to consider if you're comfortable with rates where they are right now and you don't want to constantly watch or worry about where they're going. Variable rates fluctuate with prime, so when rates go down, the interest you pay goes down too. But if rates go up, so does your interest payment. If rates are low or declining, then a variable-rate mortgage may be ideal. Variable rates may have floating payments that move with the rate, or they may have fixed payments. If the payments are fixed, then as rates drop, more of your payment is applied to principal, and if rates rise, more of the payment is applied to interest. There have been mortgages available that offer a capped interest rate on a variable-rate mortgage. This option can represent the best of both fixed- and variable-rate mortgages, because no matter how high the prime rate may rise over the term of your variable-rate mortgage, you are always protected with a fixed upper limit. It's a mortgage with a security blanket, like the Scotiabank Ultimate Variable Rate Mortgage. With most variable-rate mortgages, you have the flexibility of locking into a fixed-rate, closed-term mortgage at any time.

Now, just imagine the family dinner conversation where your brother or sister declares utter confusion at how the prime rate could drop on the same day that rates went up for fixed mortgages. This just doesn't make sense … or *does* it? Let's clarify how fixed-rate and variable-rate mortgages are priced and you'll see the difference.

Variable rates are tied to your bank's prime rate, which is based directly on the Bank of Canada rate. The Bank of Canada is our central bank, operating at arm's length from the federal government. The central bank uses its rate as a tool to achieve the goals of "low and stable inflation, a safe and secure currency, financial stability, and the efficient management of government funds and public debt." Our central bank sets the trend for short-term interest rates and has a direct impact on short-term rates for mortgages and lines of credit, as well as rates paid on deposits and investment certificates.

Fixed-term rates, such as long-term mortgage rates, by contrast, are based on the bond market. Generally, a bond is a debt with a promise to repay the principal of that debt, along with interest. Bonds are issued by governments and large businesses. We've all heard of Canada Savings Bonds, right? And they are just one type of bond. The "yield" of the bond is the annual rate of return, expressed as a percentage. Bond yields can be volatile and fluctuate in response to various political and economic factors, such as inflation and unemployment figures, and developments in the stock markets. They are increasingly affected by global forces. Long-term mortgage rates (three years and longer) are based on bond yields, but are less volatile because financial institutions absorb the daily market fluctuations in order to create a more stable rate environment for their customers. Generally speaking, higher bond yields increase funding costs for banks, which in turn leads to increased long-term fixed rates. Conversely, lower bond yields lower banks' funding costs and lead to lower long-term mortgage rates.

So, short-term rates move with the Bank of Canada's needs, while longer-term rates are tied to the bond market. The Bank of Canada can influence long-term rates, but it has no direct control over them. This difference in how rates are set is the reason we sometimes see short-term and long-term rates moving in unison, while at other times they diverge—usually around recessions. For example, when the Bank of Canada cuts rates, it usually stimulates economic recovery and growth, with the results materializing at a future point. However, in anticipation of the recovery and the associated increase in inflation, financial markets react immediately and bond yields increase. As long-term mortgage rates are priced based on bond yields, they might increase as well. That can lead to a somewhat confusing outcome where a rate cut by the Bank of Canada is followed by a decrease in variable rates and at the same time an increase in long-term fixed rates for mortgages.

Compounding interest

The way interest is calculated, in terms of the compounding frequency, is a factor in choosing the type of mortgage best for you. Most conventional fixed-rate mortgages compound interest every six months, or semi-annually. With many variable-rate mortgages, interest compounds monthly. The more often the interest compounds, the more you'll pay. So check your options. Ask your lender to compare the bottom-line value of the features and benefits and pricing of their mortgage solutions with those of the competition. And use the Internet to compare. You'll make better decisions and save money.

Does it seem as if there are just too many decisions to make when you buy a new home and have to pick a mortgage? Perhaps the easiest and best solution is to break your mortgage into a few pieces and diversify your borrowing across a range of options. For example, if you have a mortgage of $150,000, you could put half of it, or $75,000, into a fixed-rate, five-year term, for security, but split the rest in two and put $37,500 into revolving six-month terms and another $37,500 into a variable-rate mortgage with a three-year term. This is mortgage "laddering," a concept Canadians know and use to stagger their GIC maturities for diversification, but which surprisingly few of us use for our mortgages. By using this approach, you get the ultimate benefit of not having your entire mortgage exposed to one interest-rate environment at the end of the current term. You are protected, but can take advantage of shorter-term rates. Diversification is an important principle that applies as much to borrowing as it does to investing. By blending different types of mortgages and staggering maturities, you diversify your risk and minimize your interest costs. While Scotiabank offers this program, which can be a great approach, not all lenders offer this option.

Now for almost the final words on pricing ...

Be aware of introductory rates that appear to be low, but which are boosted after a very short time. Ask your lender for the actual "annual percentage rate" (APR) for the full term of your mortgage so that you know what your *real* rate of interest will be, and so that you can compare apples to apples as you assess different mortgage options. Also an important factor in mortgage pricing is your relationship with your lender, or mortgagee. Discounted mortgage rates have become a standard in the market over the past twenty years; your relationship with your lender has an impact on the size of discount you can expect to receive.

The last word on pricing is a caution: *don't let price alone determine which mortgage you choose.* It really is in your best interest to assess mortgage features against price. (You should be used to doing this in such everyday things as shopping for groceries. You know you'll pay more for prepared meals, but you'll do that if you value the time savings.) For instance, when it comes to your mortgage, the safety feature of a "capped rate" on a variable-rate mortgage can far outweigh 25 or 50 basis points on the rate. So look for quality and value in the mortgage features, not just price. Lenders have to be competitive or they won't get any business, but it's up to you to look beyond the surface.

> **Tip:** Flexible pre-payment options allow you to make more than your regular payments from time to time. The extra dollars go directly to reduce your mortgage balance and your amortization.

What Type of Mortgage Is Best for You?

Assuming that your immediate need is a home purchase, or even a renewing term, then here are the questions to start with:

- How knowledgeable are you about mortgages? Hopefully you're more knowledgeable now than when you started this book. Assuming you understand everything you have read so far, we will assess your level of knowledge as "above average" but not necessarily "expert."
- What are your borrowing goals? Ongoing access to financing? Or the ability to pay down your mortgage as fast as possible?
- Do you think you can make extra payments against your mortgage each year?
- Are you someone who almost never follows interest rates, or follows them occasionally, or very closely? The way you answer these questions helps identify your risk tolerance threshold.
- Do you know the impact of an interest-rate increase on your payments? How would you cope with higher payments?
- How long do you plan to stay in your current home? Less than two years? Three to five years? Or more than five years?

Depending upon how you respond to each of these questions determines which type of mortgage and term would be best suited to you. If you have a reasonable level of knowledge and you have some awareness of interest rates and room in your cash flow to cope with increasing (or fluctuating) interest rates, then you may want to consider a short-term or variable-rate mortgage solution. If you think you have lower risk tolerance, in that you could have difficulty with increasing rates, and if you expect to live in your home for the longer term, then a longer-term fixed-rate mortgage might let you sleep better at night.

There is one way to get the advantage of a variable-rate mortgage with an interest rate that moves with prime rate, but without all the exposure to a potentially rising-rate environment, which we have mentioned already. Ask your lender if their variable-rate mortgage has protection from rate spikes with a cap that sets a maximum interest rate you'll pay. This type of mortgage allows you to get a mortgage rate that floats with prime rate, but protects you from large interest-rate increases and the resulting higher payments.

If you think you may have access to extra cash from time to time, say, with a bonus, commission payment, or tax refund, then you should definitely look for a mortgage with built-in pre-payment flexibility. Using this type of feature can have as much or more of an impact in paying down your mortgage faster as using weekly or bi-weekly payments. Or if your income is variable throughout the year, then the ability to double up on payments at different times, but then skip a payment later provides huge flexibility with your cash flow.

If you are on the brink of taking out a new mortgage or renewing, then taking the answers to these questions to your lender can help them guide you on the best mortgage arrangement to meet your personal needs.

The Canadian Bankers Association offers a mortgage checklist

When comparison shopping, think about what features are most important to you and make a note of what each lender is offering. Here are some things to consider:

✓ types of mortgage available for the amount you need

✓ interest rate and the length of time the rate applies

✓ what the regular payment covers. Is it principal and interest only? Does it cover other costs, such as the property tax or insurance premiums the government requires?

✓ pre-payment, repayment, renegotiation and renewal options, in addition to any charges associated with them

✓ any restrictions on the home or property. Is the approval of the lender required for changes to property use while you own the property or when you're selling it?

✓ fees, if any, required by the lender in order to set up, discharge, or renew the mortgage

✓ other features, conditions and options

✓ general reputation of the lender

Some additional features and conditions may include the ability to pre-pay. If you're fortunate enough to receive an annual bonus or tax refund, you may want to consider using it to pay down your mortgage. You may be able to prepay a percentage of the original principal amount of your mortgage any time during each year of the term, though some lenders limit pre-payments to your exact anniversary date—if you miss that date, you'll have to wait until the next year. As well, once a year, you may also be able to increase the size of your regularly scheduled payment amount. All the extra dollars you pay during the term of the mortgage go directly towards the principal balance to pay down your mortgage more quickly and cut your interest expense. Some lenders offer the ability to double up on a regular payment, on any scheduled payment date without fees or early-repayment penalties. This can generate great flexibility for you if the lender also offers a "skip a payment" option. If occasionally you find that your cash flow is a bit snug, then you may be able to miss a payment, up to the value of any additional mortgage payments you've made during that term. These are important features to check out, for they can have much greater value over the long term than a discount on your mortgage rate.

Bottom line: not all mortgages are the same. And having the right mortgage for you can make your house seem more like a home—more comfortable and secure. For a quick reference and more complete list of mortgage and borrowing terms, refer to the Glossary at the end of the book.

Take advantage of mortgage pre-payment options:

This table shows the advantages of mortgage pre-payment options on a mortgage of $100,000 with an interest rate of 6%

	No pre-payments	Single 15% pre-payment made at the beginning of the first year of the mortgage	Monthly payments increased by 15%
Monthly Payment	$639.81	$639.81	$735.78
Years to pay off mortgage	25 years	18 years, 1 month	18 years, 10 months
Estimated interest savings over life of the mortgage	N/A	$38,312.51	$25,810.80

When to break the contract: refinance, blend and extend, early renewal

With interest rates continuing to bounce around the bottom of historically low levels, much discussion has been prompted around early-renewal options. Breaking a set mortgage contract is not an entirely straightforward transaction. After all, it is a contract with benefits and responsibilities on both sides of the commitment. That said, you still may have options, so read the fine print on the mortgage agreement you signed with your lender, and let's clarify the following issues:

An *open mortgage* is totally open and subject to early payout or refinance without penalties. Open mortgages generally come with higher rates for the benefit you have of early payout or refinance. A popular form of open mortgage has been variable-rate mortgages tied to the prime rate. Though not all "prime rate" mortgages are "open." You need to know what you signed up for.

A *closed mortgage* is just that: closed. It represents a commitment between you and your mortgagee for the term of the mortgage. With a closed mortgage, the homeowner gets the commitment from the lender that there will be no change to interest rates or payment amounts for the term of the agreement even if rates go up. You agree, however, to make your payments over the term of the commitment, subject to any early-repayment options that may be built-in to the contract. While the closed mortgage is set, there may be options for early renewal, but at a price.

Early renewal is the process of breaking the term of your existing contract and setting a new term with a new interest rate and payment amount. The penalty most often applied for early renewal is a three-month interest payment, which is calculated based on your current mortgage balance at your current interest rate over three months. The other common early-renewal penalty is called "interest rate differential" (IRD). The IRD is the difference between the interest rate in your mortgage contract and the current lending rates over the remaining period of your mortgage. And the early-renewal cost is most often calculated to be the greater of the IRD or the three-month interest rate penalty, depending on how far you are into your mortgage term.

Some lenders provide a *blend or extend* option. This sounds attractive in that you're taking the interest obligation of your existing mortgage and blending it with a lower current rate, and then extending your term at the lower, blended rate. And there is no interest penalty. But you are still paying the obligation you made in the existing contract. You're just creating a lower rate, and payment, by using the weighted interest cost between the existing contract and the new term. If it works and you can save money and benefit from lower rates for longer, then that's great!

> **Tip:** If you believe that interest rates are increasing, arrange for an early renewal before maturity and lock in at a lower rate to avoid possible payment increases.

Many people contend that they should be given a discounted rate for early renewal because they could get a deeply discounted competitor rate if they shopped around. But people often forget that their contract is "closed" for a certain term. They are not in the same position to "shop" for their mortgage as they were originally or will be at the end of each term.

If you have been in a relatively long-term mortgage and are within six months of the current term maturing, then your lender may give you the flexibility to renew early without any penalties or conditions—but this depends on the lender and, typically, the overall relationship you have with your lender. If you think rates are low and your mortgage is close to renewal time, then have a chat with your lender about your options.

If you plan to switch your mortgage to a new lender, then the conversation will be entirely different. What interest penalty amount should you expect as the "exit cost" from your contract? A payout penalty, as described above, is calculated based on the greater of the IRD and a three-month interest penalty. If the mortgage is within the first three years of set-up, then there may also be an administration fee applied that could be as much as about $200. There will also be a mortgage-discharge fee applied of $150 to $180. Then, if you received Cashback as part of your benefit at the beginning of the mortgage term, then the lender will recover the Cashback on a pro-rated basis—this is referred to as the *clawback* provision on Cashback. And you may have to pay legal costs and mortgage registration fees to set up the new mortgage with a new lender. This is not an inexpensive proposition, so do the math! The closer you are to the end of your term, the lower the cost. Otherwise, there needs to be a pretty big drop in rates between what you're booked at currently and what you think you can get to make an early payout and switch to another lender to save money.

Refinancing Your Mortgage

If you want to refinance your mortgage, because you need money to finance a project or to purchase another property, there are relatively efficient ways to do this now available to homeowners in most provinces. If you don't think you need legal advice on the transaction, then there are programs offered by some lenders that can provide a cost-effective way to refinance mortgage debt on either residential or farm properties, without the direct involvement of a lawyer. An existing, registered mortgage debt may be refinanced using *instant funding* at maturity or in the middle of your term. Instant funding (which requires title insurance) allows funds to be advanced to the borrower immediately on signing the mortgage documents, either in a branch or another convenient location. A great service available at a reasonable cost to discharge and re-register mortgage documents while advancing funds quickly, instant funding can often be the answer when you see your dream cottage or country home come onto the market, or you finally make the decision to add an addition.

When does instant funding not work? While most situations are straightforward and instant funding is an option, there are always exceptions, including the following, where instant funding is not available:

- new purchase transactions
- progress draws for construction or renovation mortgages
- when a power of attorney is involved for any of the borrowers
- when any borrower is a corporation
- if title to the property is changing (e.g., adding, deleting or changing a name)
- if there is an estate on title.

Always check with your lender if you're contemplating a significant need for cash. There may be a range of interesting and appropriate options available to you.

Bridge Loan

A *bridge loan* is a special borrowing solution for customers involved in real estate purchases and sales. It offers a short-term financing option to home buyers who want to buy a new home but haven't closed on the sale of their current home.

How does a bridge loan work? You can usually take up to about three months to complete the sale of your existing property, after you have already closed on the purchase of your new home. This can offer tremendous peace of mind if you've found the home of your dreams but have only just listed your existing home for sale. Or it can offer real flexibility if you need to make improvements and repairs on your new home before you move in. Sometimes it's just nice to stagger your closing dates by just a few days or a week so that you can give the new house a thorough cleaning before the movers arrive. A bridge loan can get you even a few days of flexibility. And then you repay the loan, with interest, when the sale of your existing home is complete.

Need a little more detail? If you think you're carrying two full mortgages for the bridging period, it's really not that overwhelming. You are only borrowing the value of the equity in your existing home, since the rest of the funds you need are already advanced in your new mortgage. And you will be applying the value of that equity to your new home as soon as the existing home is sold. So this is a relatively low-cost, temporary financing arrangement to give you some flexibility. An example might be helpful:

> **Sandor and Alya** are now ready to buy their new house for $300,000. They will need a first mortgage for $150,000. Of the remaining $150,000, they are contributing $30,000 from their own savings. The remaining $120,000 will come from the net proceeds on the sale of their existing home. Since everything except that $120,000 is available, when Sandor and Alya are ready to close on the new house, they will need to bridge-finance $120,000 for a few months.
>
> And here is what they will pay. At most financial institutions, the set-up or administrative fee is about $250. The typical interest rate is about prime plus 2%. So Sandor and Alya can expect to pay about 6.5% interest (assuming prime is 4.5%) on $120,000 for three months, plus fees, which will add up to about $2,200.

Caution: To arrange a bridge loan, lenders usually require two firm offers (any conditions have to be satisfied), one for the old house and one for the new property. This requirement can make it difficult to get bridge financing if you have bought the new house without selling your existing home. Be very aware of your options before you go out and buy a new house without selling the old one! This is where a "conditional upon financing" clause may be critical.

What If I'm Building a New House?

If you're building a new house and you need a mortgage to fund the construction, then a *progress advance mortgage* is used by most lenders. This is a mortgage that is funded in stages, based on the total building cost and the rate at which work is completed. Before you begin construction, you should ask your lender for an estimate of the amounts that you can expect to receive as work progresses. That estimate will let you better understand the advance process, manage your cash flow requirements, and properly plan the project with your builder.

What If I'm Buying a New House from a Builder?

If you're buying a brand-new house from a builder, you may be able to take advantage of attractive mortgage rates available from an on-site lender. The mortgage interest rates offered through builders are generally very competitive and are often made available for an extended period of time, usually until you take possession of your new home. Since construction deadlines may be missed (in fact, are missed more often than not), mortgages offered through the builder can provide protection against rising interest rates if your possession date is delayed, since the builder may guarantee the rate until closing. You should still do your homework, though. Make sure you read the fine print in the builder's mortgage agreement. Of course, comparing all your options with the options your personal banker offers will ensure that you're getting the best mortgage solution for your needs.

Financing Your Renovation

For many Canadians, rising real estate prices, combined with low interest rates, have made home renovation a compelling alternative to moving. Renovation is an especially attractive option if you like your neighbours and the amenities of your current home. In fact, Statistics Canada and CMHC report that Canadians are now spending more than $30 billion a year on home repairs, improvements, and renovations, with homeowners in British Columbia and Quebec heading the pack. Now you know why so many home-renovation-supply stores are popping up on the landscape!

Whether you're thinking about finishing a basement, adding another floor, or tackling a leaky old bathroom, here are a few basics tips to keep in mind before you embark on your home-renovation project:

- Check municipal building regulations. Building regulations vary from municipality to municipality. It's important that you understand how your intended renovation project fits with your local building by-laws. Before beginning, find out what building permits you will require from your municipal offices.
- Be realistic about the size of your project. Whether you intend to complete the renovation yourself or you hire a contractor, it's important to plan your project carefully. It's especially important if you can't live in your home for a while during the work, since living elsewhere can get very expensive. Make sure you have enough time and money to complete the job.
- Do some homework before you hire a contractor. If you hire a professional contractor for your renovation project, it's important that you are comfortable with the contractor's ability to complete the job. Ask around. Friends, family, and neighbours can be a good resource when looking for a contractor. If a contractor has done satisfactory work of similar design and construction on a neighbour's home, you might use him, since there may be fewer surprises. And be sure to check a potential contractor's refer-

ences; contractors are usually happy to offer a few. And it's always a good idea to check out the contractor with the Better Business Bureau.

- Don't overextend yourself. With interest rates as low as they have been, renovation has been a good option for homeowners, but for financing, talk with your lender about what works best for you, whether it's a personal line of credit, refinancing of your mortgage, or a more comprehensive borrowing solution. However you choose to finance the project, be realistic about the amount that you can borrow and your ability to repay. That may mean doing part of the work yourself or breaking down the project into separate parts, which you tackle one at a time as you can comfortably afford.

It's important to protect the value of your investment. So get organized before you approach any renovation project.

The Canadian Home Builders Association reports the following trends in home renovation:

Multi-generational housing, whether it's to accommodate children staying at home longer or aging parents.

Accessible housing features, including minor adjustments such as lever-type door handles, grab-bars and non-skid flooring.

The home office, with built-in workstations, shelving, and storage space.

Home-entertainment centres, with all the electronic gadgetry, plus acoustical insulation and custom-built shelving.

Energy retrofitting, from insulation to energy-efficient heating systems, windows, appliances, and lighting, which can all be upgraded to reduce your energy bills.

Improving the air quality in your home with a ventilation system or products to minimize air-borne pollution.

Home security, with perimeter and interior motion alarm systems to improve the safety of your family and your belongings.

Credit Insurance

As perhaps your largest investment, your home should be protected for your family. While we don't believe in being over-insured because of the expense, it is important to have enough insurance coverage to protect your family if you become ill or die. *Creditor insurance* can be an affordable way to provide protection. More specifically, the most commonly used form of creditor insurance is "loss of life protection," which will pay the principal and interest remaining on your mortgage should you as the mortgagor die before the mortgage is paid out.

There are other types of creditor insurance that have been introduced in the past ten years for homeowners with a mortgage. One is "health crisis protection." This coverage is a "living benefit" and will pay off your mortgage balance if you suffer a specific and previously cited health crisis. For example, if you suffer a stroke or a heart attack, your mortgage will be paid off (whether or not you are still able to work), and you can focus on getting healthy again.

Creditor insurance premiums are calculated based on your age and the amount of coverage you're considering (which is the mortgage balance outstanding at the time of the application). The younger you are when you apply, the lower your premiums will be. Check your bank's web site for more information.

Mortgage Life Insurance is a particularly important option to consider. It's a wise choice if you are young and have financial responsibilities that could be a burden on your family without your income. Even if you have no dependants, mortgage life insurance would ensure that the mortgage is covered while your estate is being settled. If you are already covered by a stand-alone insurance plan, then you may have enough life insurance—only you know. Some people like to structure their insurance so that the mortgage life insurance clears their debt, covering the reducing amount of their mortgage balance, while also having a stand-alone policy to help with income replacement. If you need other coverage beyond your mortgage amount, be sure to talk to an insurance company.

Credit Reports, Ratings, and Scores

If you're thinking that this section sounds rather boring and maybe you'll just skip it, do yourself a favour and read on. This is an important part of your portfolio of knowledge.

- Many Canadians admit they don't know what a credit report is or how it works.
- Yet almost all of us borrow, so this is something you really should understand. You don't want any nasty surprises with the interest rate you pay on your credit card next month!

We'll even offer a few good tips on how you can improve your credit score.

The credit bureau

Before we get to credit ratings and credit scores, which seem very mysterious, let's understand the credit bureau. In the early settlements across North America, local merchants who operated the general store were granting credit to customers, and they kept track of obligations with small handwritten notes. But by the mid-1800s, as communities grew and merchants sprang up around the general store, a need developed to share the notes from the general store so that all credit grantors could make more informed credit-granting decisions. Someone decided to collect these notes, or records, and hold them centrally for all credit grantors to access. This was the beginning of credit bureaus.

A number of innovations have advanced the role of the credit bureau. When the typewriter became widely available, credit reports were more accurate, or at least more easily read. And carbon paper allowed for easier copying and sharing of information. As technology advanced and computers became host to data files, and then the modem was launched (even in its most primitive form 25 years ago), dial-up access to information made the system more efficient, and the earliest faxes were sent expediently to prospective credit grantors. Then as technology evolved further, credit bureaus were able to provide assistance in a broader range of financial transactions. Today, the process bears little resemblance to the bits of paper gathered by a general-store clerk for reference. Information can be now shared globally and is passed so instantly that business decisions can be made in seconds or minutes rather than days or weeks. With on-line access, credit grantors can easily provide regular updates to the credit bureau to ensure that your file is current. And the credit bureau can be more responsive to inquiries. The information that is shared extends not only to credit-granting transactions, but also helps with identification of potential frauds to protect your financial transactions. So credit bureaus have become a well-entrenched part of consumer and commercial financial transactions.

Today in Canada, there are two major credit bureaus: Equifax and Trans Union. They are global organizations, and they operate here according to our legislative and regulatory framework. Equifax has operated for almost a

hundred years and declares its commitment "to providing superior information protection practices worthy of the public's trust." Confidence in integrity
and privacy practices is paramount in the operation of a credit bureau today,
both from the perspective of consumers and the businesses that participate in
information sharing. We all depend on organizations like Equifax and Trans
Union to provide timely, accurate, and relevant information for risk assessment, and they acknowledge this expectation. So rest assured that the most
advanced technologies are in place to safeguard your information.

Well, that's all very interesting, but why should we really care about credit
bureaus? Every day there are millions of financial transactions completed across
the country as people present credit cards in bookstores and dress shops, as
they buy a car, apply for jobs, go apartment hunting, or set up telephone and
other utilities in the home they just purchased. While these might not all seem
like financial transactions, in almost every case the granting of credit takes
place. Even the utility that provides power to your home bills you after you
have taken delivery of the service and anticipates payment within the following
month. Your telephone and power providers are granting credit; they want
some assurance that you'll pay the bills. And so, credit grantors rely on the
credit bureau to get a credit report or a credit score before they grant credit.

What is a credit report?

A credit report is a record of all your credit activity, including details of all
transactions over the prior six years. A credit report is established in your
name the very first time you apply for credit and is updated regularly for as
long as you have credit. The report not only captures problematic situations,
but also good repayment experience. It includes the following details:

• applications for credit and inquiries from credit grantors
• current loans and credit cards from banks, finance companies, and retailers
• details on each account: when they were opened, balances, and payments
• personal information that will help to identify you specifically, including
  your name, address, and date of birth
• a list of "inquiries," which is everyone who has requested your credit
  report over the past three years
• a list of any bankruptcy, judgement, or collection agency involvement if
  you have ever had a problem with your credit
• a "consumer statement," which is an optional comment that you can add
  to your own credit report that helps to explain a situation to prospective
  credit grantors. For example, if you were ill and unable to work for a few
  months, then you may have had temporary difficulty paying bills, and you
  can share this information in the consumer statement section.

Check out the web site for Equifax Canada for more helpful information and resources on your credit report at www.equifax.ca. Here's an introduction to what they have to say:

Your credit report is important to you. Yet many Canadians have never looked at their own credit report, so it's not surprising that it is often overlooked when individuals assess their financial situation.

The Consumer Information Centre has been designed to inform you about credit reporting in general, and more specifically, how to obtain a copy of your credit report and **ensure it is accurate**. You can consult **Frequently Asked Questions**, which cover many aspects of consumer credit reporting in addition to **Other Topics & Resources**, where you'll find useful tips about credit ratings and counselling, among other subjects. And we've included **Helpful Links** to other information sources about credit reporting in general.

If you would like to obtain a copy of your credit report immediately, for a fee, you can receive real-time on-line access to your personal credit report, credit score and a full explanation of your score and how lenders view your credit history. Simply log on to Equifax Consumer Services Canada at **www.econsumer.equifax.ca.**

To obtain a free copy of your credit report by mail, go to **Your Credit Report** and download the credit report request form. You can also access your credit report at TransUnion's website at **www.tuc.ca.**

You can and should ask for a copy of your own credit report and see what it says about you to ensure that it is current and accurate.

Who else can see your credit report? Well, the credit report is available to subscribers. It is only available with your consent. And it can only be provided in the following situations: where credit is being granted, or for collection purposes; by prospective landlords when you apply for a house or apartment rental; by employers; and for insurance purposes. Yes, even insurers want to know that you'll pay your premiums. When you are granted credit, your lender may continue to request your credit bureau information from time to time to update their records. And the report will not include any comments from credit grantors, only the detailed facts of your identity, your borrowing experience, and if you have included one, your consumer statement.

You may have heard of a *credit score* or a *credit rating*, which are different from a credit report, but integral to it. A credit *rating* is an indicator used to rank the quality of your repayment on each and every loan or credit card you hold. Credit ratings range on a scale from R0 to R9, where R0 means there is not enough information to have a rating and R9 is an indication of bad debt. The ratings from R1 to R8 represent everything in between; for example, R1 shows that you pay everything on time for that account and R5 means your account may have been overdue for four months. Ideally, you really don't want anything other than a list of R1s appearing on your credit report, but we are only human and have been known to overlook a bill from time to time, like the one that got mixed in with the stack of your five-year-old's kindergarten artwork on the counter in the kitchen. Or the one that disappeared that month you moved, and what little control you normally maintain over your family's life was shot. Don't panic if you've had a similar experience: the rare R2 or R3 won't ruin your life.

While a credit rating is assigned to every account, a credit *score* is a summary of all the data in your credit report, reflecting your overall borrowing behaviour. Not every lender wants or needs an entire credit report from the credit bureau, and a score, which can be a three-digit number, serves as an adequate gauge of your credit worthiness. There are lots of different approaches to scoring, but they're all used for the same purpose: to help a lender make a decision on whether to approve credit or grant credit-limit increases. Part of the score can be made of the total amount of your debt, part is the level of usage as a percentage of available credit limits, part is the length of your credit history, and the biggest part is usually your payment history. Depending on the credit bureau and the scoring model it uses, the score may be called a FICO score by Fair Isaacs, a Beacon score by Equifax, or an Empirica score by TransUnion. For reference, the higher the score, the better, with a score over 700 being good, and a score under 640 indicating problems. While this offers a general guideline, every lender still determines their own level of risk tolerance. And many lenders even create their proprietary scoring models to capture a broader range of variables to help with their credit-risk management. For example, at Scotiabank, we recognize the deposits and investments you may have with us, which, based on our experience, strengthen the overall likelihood you'll be a good credit risk and repay. We blend that information with the credit bureau score to create our own credit score for our customers.

Because **Karen** has been paying off her student loan and enjoying life in Vancouver, she has not yet saved any money for a down payment.
She has a line of credit that she avoids using, but keeps her three credit cards at the top of her wallet for nights out and shopping. One

of the three cards has a very low interest rate, but the other two, which she uses to collect points, have rates at over 18%. She tries to pay those cards off each month, but often carries a balance. She pays her balances off in full at least once a year.

Karen is having fun and has been spending her money. While she has no savings, she has been living well within her means. As a result, her credit report looks very clean. Here is what it says: "Your FICO Credit Score is 790."

By any measure, this is an excellent score, and a credit bureau report might say the following: "Lenders would consider this to be an excellent score. Other factors, such as income and capacity, may be considered when making a credit decision, but looking solely at your FICO score, lenders would have no concerns granting credit to this customer."

Karen is likely to be approved for any reasonable credit request, and she will have access to that credit at the best rates available.

Maria and John consistently pay all their bills on time every month, so their credit ratings are all R1. They've had credit cards and student loans since they were at university, so there is enough of a track record for a lender to have confidence in their repayment. But to manage with a young family, a new house, a new car, and a line of credit to cope with some expenses on the house, they have taken on a very high level of debt relative to their income. And they have just bought all the appliances for their new home at a store where they signed up for the "Don't pay until …" deal, which will mean even more payments when those commitments come due. Maria and John are okay, but they are a bit squeezed on cash flow.

When they requested a copy of their credit report recently, they found the following comments:

"Your FICO Credit Score is 745. Lenders consider many factors in addition to your credit score when making credit decisions. Looking solely at your FICO score, however, most lenders would consider this score as good."

So it is improbable that any additional request for credit would be declined based on their score. In fact, Maria and John qualified for their unsecured line of credit at prime plus 1.5% based on the quality of their score. As they pay down their debt and their credit score rises, they may qualify for an even more preferential rate. They could be declined for additional credit, depending on the amount, if they don't have enough capacity in their cash flow to make the payments while meeting existing obligations.

Sandor and Alya have divided responsibility for bill payments between the two of them. While they both have the money in their account to be able to pay their bills on time every month, they sometimes get distracted by their lives and lose track. The confusion is often compounded when one of them thinks that the other had paid a bill when the other didn't, so it's only when the overdue notice comes in that they realize they missed something.

This inconsistency in repayment has affected their credit report, and this is what it says: "Your FICO Credit Score is 650. Lenders might have some apprehension about this score. This score would indicate that there has been some credit delinquency in the past. Other factors will be considered by lenders in making their decision, but this FICO score may or may not be acceptable based upon the risk tolerance level of the specific lender."

While Sandor and Alya may be approved for credit, because they do ultimately pay all their bills and because they have capacity, they will likely pay a higher interest rate than they should have to, based on their confusion in managing day-to-day bills.

Since payment history is stored by credit bureaus for six years, Sandor and Alya's report could start to improve if they just coordinate better on payments, and make them on time.

Interestingly, a credit report does not include information on perhaps the most significant borrowing that most of us ever do: your mortgage. So far, your mortgage size and repayment information is not shared with other creditors. But that's all about to change. It is expected that in the next two years, mortgage information will be shared, and then the file is relatively complete. In most cases, your government student loans are reported to the credit bureau too. So if you ever thought that you don't really have to repay the government that loan they gave you for your education in 1995 (or for your Reading Week vacation in Florida), think again. That debt could haunt you for quite a while. Bottom line, a good credit rating will stand you in good terms with a lender who is reviewing your mortgage or borrowing application. As for unsecured credit, a better credit score will generally work to your benefit there as well.

While credit reporting has become totally automated, that automation has its advantages and disadvantages. Let's start with the downside. In spite of the enormous benefits of automation, there is one key drawback: people who have no credit history have trouble *getting* credit, and it's more challenging than ever for lenders to extend credit to such people, usually young people and new immigrants, as well as people emerging from a marriage breakdown who have never had credit in their own name (most often women). Most lenders recognize this issue as a significant drawback, so banks tend to have good exception-handling processes. For new immigrants, your bank may offer a special program. Scotiabank offers a "Welcome to Canada" package, which handles credit decision-making differently. And for students, we encourage young people to apply with their parents as co-borrowers. By having parents sign up on your first car loan or student loan, young people get the advantage of their parents' more developed credit rating—hopefully the parents' credit rating is good, which may mean a better interest rate! The same applies for anyone who has never had credit. Have a chat with a personal banker at your branch, and chances are you can get approved at least for a small amount of credit. Once you're established a good repayment track record, then the bene- fits of credit reporting work in your favour.

On the upside of automation in credit reporting are three strong benefits:

1. *Better information.* With enormous capacity for data collection, the credit bureau is equipped to capture a more comprehensive and, as a result, more reliable picture of your credit history. Plus, your report is updated regularly, so if your situation changes (for the better or worse), that will quickly be reflected in the information that is shared.

2. *Faster decisions.* Credit-granting decisions can be made in seconds with rapid exchange of information through the credit bureau and lender systems, whether you're at a car dealership wanting a car loan or hoping for approval on a mortgage for the home of your dreams that just came up for sale.

3. *Objective decisions.* In the day when everyone knew everyone in their community, risk assessment was managed at a personal level, leaving room for the risk of discrimination across a range of variables. Your uncle's posi- tion in town no longer has any bearing on credit decision-making. Now everyone applying for credit is on a level playing field.

Key conclusion: Always, always, always pay your bills on time.

Don't think that just paying your bills every month is good enough. You need to consistently pay them by the due date. A customer from Calgary called recently with concern that the interest rate on her line of credit appli- cation had gone up since she started the application a few months ago. We asked a few questions about her bill payments over those months to deter- mine if her credit score might have deteriorated, and she related how difficult it is to make ends meet. We certainly understood and were fully sympathetic. But with a little more probing she revealed that "the first pay of the month is for the mortgage and the second pay covers something else, and the third pay is for the bills." But the problem was that her phone and hydro and credit card bills were all due in the middle of each month, and she was late every single month—and paid extra interest for that. If she had just turned around the priorities so that second pay was used for bills, then her credit rating wouldn't have been so impaired.

One option that may have worked for that customer could have been to ask her utility companies to put her on a billing cycle in which payments were due later in the month. If things aren't quite so straightforward, here's another option: sign up for on-line banking. It's secure and easy. Your bank will be happy to give you a demonstration. Set up all your bill payments to be paid just a few days before the due date. Then get overdraft protection, or ODP (some banks have a better service than others in terms of fees and rates, so check around). With ODP, you're covered between pay periods for those bill payments. You can pay a lot for ODP, so look for the best offer and set up your day-to-day banking with that financial institution.

No computer? Same idea applies to telephone banking. Or set up pre-authorized payments. And as for writing cheques, get all your cheques ready when you sit down once a month to do the bills, then on the back of each envelope, discreetly write the date that the envelope should go in the mail to arrive on time. Then just get to that mailbox on time!

If you have tried to skip this section because you think it's boring, stop and read on. You really should know about this part!

Okay, so this section may have been a bit dry. For those of you who forged through it and gained some new insight, well done. For everyone else who tried to skip this section, we recommend that you pause and focus on this part. There is just so much confusion out there about how credit ratings and scores are developed and used. And what we've set out so far covers the basics. But this really is a big deal because **your credit rating will determine how much you pay in interest for borrowing.** A good credit rating can get you better rates, particularly on unsecured borrowing. Here's how credit pricing works: it's based on risk. And risk is predicated on the "three Cs," which all lenders know well: character, capacity, and collateral. Character is your repayment history, capacity is how much income you have to support the debt repayment, and collateral is the security you pledge against the loan. If you have a pristine repayment history and you have enough income to support the credit, and you use your home to secure the borrowing, you will most likely get the lowest interest rates available on borrowing from your lender at the time the account is set up. If you have an unsecured line of credit or credit card, and your repayment behaviour deteriorates (even with another lender) then the credit score will change to reflect the change in your behaviour, and the lender may have the option to put up the interest rate on your credit to reflect their recognition of a new higher level of risk. If you are chronically late or skip payments, then while you may be easing your cash flow challenges for today, you're making them more difficult down the road.

If you anticipate a need to borrow and know that a lender is likely to look at your credit report, or at least your credit score, here are a few things you can do to maintain a positive credit rating or improve your position:

- Above all, always pay your bills on time! (Have we mentioned this already?)
- Try not to operate with your revolving credit at the maximum credit limit.
- Try to pay down your balances to below 75% of the credit limit, and this should improve your score.
- Check your credit report annually to ensure there are no errors.
- Manage how many inquiries are made against your file. The more inquiries that are made for credit applications, the more your score will be impaired.
- If you have had no credit in the past, but have made regular contributions into a savings plan, then this program can demonstrate an established pattern of repayment capability. Be prepared to demonstrate this pattern to your lender.

By following these guidelines, you'll be sure to have better access to the credit you deserve, and you'll have access to that credit at the lowest possible interest rates.

Identity fraud

Just before we leave our discussion on credit, we need to acknowledge a tremendous consumer service contribution to fighting identity theft and fraud. For example, TransUnion has been working on this issue for more than ten years with its Fraud Victim Assistance Department. Check out their web site at **www.tuc.ca** to see what they have to say about this growing concern.

Welcome to TransUnion's Fraud Victim Assistance Department (FVAD). We recognize that being a victim of identity fraud, or potentially being exposed to fraud through a lost or stolen wallet, can be a stressful, upsetting experience. Our service is here to help you register the incident and identify if any fraudulent credit activity has occurred. Our objective is to make this experience as comfortable as possible for you, providing important guidance and information to help you rectify any fraud activity that has occurred involving your identity.

Please review our Frequently Asked Fraud Questions to find answers that will:

• Provide guidance if you suspect or know you are a victim of identity fraud

• Provide suggestions on how to avoid becoming a victim of fraud

• The signs can vary, but typical indicators of fraud include:

• A creditor's fraud department informs you that an application for credit was received with your name and address, for which you did not apply.

• Telephone calls or letters state that you have been approved or denied by a creditor to which you never applied.

• You receive credit card statements or other bills in your name, for which you did not apply.

• You no longer receive credit card statements or notice that not all of your mail is delivered.

• A collection agency informs you that they are collecting for a defaulted account established with your identity and you never opened the account.

CHAPTER 8

The Four Fundamentals of a Borrowing Strategy

Now let's help you be a better borrower. If you can take only four things from this book, then let them be these fundamentals. Maybe they'll help you sleep a little more soundly, or you might even be able to save a few dollars for your children's education, or even pay off your borrowing a bit faster. For these four fundamentals will allow you to be a better borrower without leaving your comfort zone.

The Four Fundamentals

1. Do a rigorous self-assessment

Self-assessment of your needs and wants is the key to smart borrowing. Start by setting out your personal financial goals. Rank them in priority. Think about them a little more and categorize them as "needs" or "wants" and then force-rank each list. Here are some ideas to get you started:

- Think about big, long-term goals around your ownership of a home or homes (if you want a cottage or chalet).
- Think about your children (if you have them or plan to): orthodontics and summer camp, and consider their education.
- Do you want to lower your monthly payments or reduce your borrowing costs?
- Are you concerned about retiring comfortably? While the mandatory retirement age may be eliminated or raised, you still may want to reach for the flexibility of retirement or partial retirement at some point.
- Do you need to be prepared in case you face an emergency? How long can you manage to cover the day-to-day expenses if your income drops (if you get sick or lose your job)?

Then consider some more immediate, perhaps less overwhelming goals:
- Would you like to take a small vacation in Old Montreal or on a beach? Maybe a few days skiing outside Calgary?
- Are you planning a home renovation? Or just some new paint and a few new windows?

- When will you need a new car? Are you a two-vehicle household that needs to update both?

When you've done your ranking, look at the borrowing scenarios that best fit into your personal comfort zone.

- Are you managing on a tight cash flow that would be sensitive to payment increases due to interest rate changes?
- Do you have a bit of extra room each month that you can divide between savings and more repayment of borrowing?
- Do you want simple financing for a one-time major purchase?
- Do you want the flexibility of being able to access financing on an ongoing basis?

Now assess what your income is likely to be over the next few years.

- Do you expect cost-of-living increases? Or perhaps a bit more?
- Will your income vary with commissions or bonuses?

Generally, get a good picture of where you are now, and where you want to be.

2. Get organized

Now you need to review your expenses and see where you can make cuts if need be. Take your papers out of the shoebox and put pen to paper. Better yet, set up a spreadsheet (this is obviously easier if you have a computer). Categorize the essential non-negotiables and the discretionary or even extravagant items. Use the table in Appendix B to help. Set up this spreadsheet so you can see how much money comes in and where the money goes every month. Take off the blinders and really look—the high-end food store as opposed to the corner grocery, the exclusive car wash as opposed to the do-it-yourself job. … Everyone who does this is usually very surprised, and better equipped to make some changes to discretionary expenses. It might be as simple as turning off the satellite dish for a few months. Maybe you won't miss the extra cable channels when the weather changes.

3. Simplify around your goals

Once you know where you are and you've organized, you can simplify. Life is busy for all of us, and while this will take a little work, you'll benefit.

Reduce the number of credit cards that you carry. You don't necessarily need to close accounts. Just take some of the cards out of your wallet and put them in a safe place. Most people do best to have one card to use for day-to-day purchases and collecting points, along with one lower rate option when they need to carry a balance. But everyone is different, so look at what you need. (Or if you'll be charged a fee because they are inactive, which is increasingly common, think of getting rid of some cards.)

Ideally, this is where you set up an appointment with your banker or financial adviser to consider how you can simplify your borrowing around your goals. Apply the same approach and principles to borrowing that you would to investing to improve your cash flow (by reducing your overall cost of borrowing), and mitigate exposure to interest rate risks with diversification, as we've discussed already.

4. Optimize your homeownership experience

The process of homeownership is long. It's emotional, intellectual, and even physical. You need to live with and be comfortable with your home. So, invest when you are ready. Stay aware of your cash flow. And, recognize how your environment may be changing (and the impact that may have on you).

Leverage your home equity to reduce your overall cost of borrowing, and then *pay the debt off.* When you create some room in your cash flow by reducing your cost of borrowing, use that cash to pay down debt. You'll be in a better position to cope should interest rates move up.

Manage your homeownership costs. Keep heating bills down with simple tips from your heating services provider. Enbridge claims you can save up to 9% of your natural gas use by "sealing cracks and drafts around windows, doors and electrical sockets." For one family we know, who live in a century-old farmhouse and consume more than $2,000 worth of gas a year, that could make a real difference. Even if your home is well insulated, you can have a significant saving in energy costs by reducing the temperature setting on the thermostat by just a few degrees before you leave for work every day.

Finally, appreciate and enjoy what you have—you've worked hard for it! Use your borrowing strategy to get you to a situation that works for you.

Where Do I Go from Here?

You've read all the directions, digested the examples, and been through the checklists. Now you ask, "Where do I go from here?" To help you embark on your personal journey, this final section points you to your key next steps. You can approach this in one of two ways: call the local branch of your bank and ask for an appointment with a personal banker; or do a little groundwork over the Internet and do some personalized calculations to get you closer to identifying your comfort zone. Of course, it's not a bad idea to do both.

If you opt for only the meeting with the banker, then here is how you might approach it. Begin by framing your personal goals, your financial goals, and your worries. Write them down. It doesn't have to be a long list, but by writing down a few key thoughts, you have a good place to start the conversation. In the meeting, you can ask for the banker's help in framing your borrowing strategy. Your banker should have the tools to guide you through a helpful discussion.

For research on the Internet, see Selected Web Sites, page 119. If you'll indulge us again here for a minute, we'll put our Scotiabank hats back on and use our resources and tools as the examples to guide you.

At **www.scotiabank.com**, check the Mortgage Centre for tools that can help you. We really like the mortgage payment calculator called *"Calculate how much your mortgage payments might be."* It can instantly calculate your mortgage payment based on the amount and interest rate you input. Keep in mind that this is just the principal and interest payment; it does not include taxes or creditor insurance. But it still offers a solid indication of the range of mortgage you can carry. The other calculator we like is called *"How much might I qualify for?"* which essentially does a Total Debt Service Ratio calculation with very little input required. You can get an idea from this of the amount of mortgage (or overall borrowing) for which you might be approved. If you take a look at these tools before you meet with a lender, then your conversation can be even more focused, and you'll approach it with greater confidence.

Our all-time favourite tool is the STEP Worksheet on the Scotiabank web site. If you own a home and you have borrowed money on credit cards or unsecured lines of credit, or you have a car loan, then this tool can show you how you can save on your overall cost of borrowing. As we've said, the Scotia Total Equity Plan is a bundled borrowing solution, combining your mortgage, lines of credit, VISA cards, personal loans, business loans, and overdrafts. It uses the equity in your home to reduce your overall cost of borrowing. By identifying all your borrowing and the interest rate you are currently paying, the STEP Worksheet will run the calculation for you of how much you could save in interest costs by converting all your borrowing into one collateral mortgage program. You may be amazed at how much you can save and how much closer you can get to meeting your financial goals. You'll find this tool works best if you have your credit card and loan statements in hand. Using the most accurate information will give you the best indication of how much of an improvement you can make to get you on track to being a better borrower.

Even if you started out with your own Internet research, it still makes sense to plan a visit with your lender. They'll have even more resources, experience, and insight to help you make sound decisions, as well as provide you with the tools to help guide you on the best type of mortgage to fit your comfort zone. At Scotiabank, we have a homeownership selector that can simplify the process of finding the right mortgage options for you. And then our comparison tool can actually show you how different bank mortgages stack up against each other on features and benefits. Don't fall for the old misperception that "a mortgage is a mortgage is a mortgage" and all banks are the same. There are big differences, some of which can have an impact on you. Since your mortgage is likely to be the biggest financial decision you'll make, approach it well armed with accurate, current information.

In Conclusion ...

If you were feeling uneasy about home buying and mortgages before you embarked on this book, we trust you feel less anxious now. At the very least, you should walk away with a better sense of the critical role that your home has in your life as an investment, how to make a good investment, how to protect that investment, and how to use it to be a better borrower. We hope that you can approach your lender more confidently in the future, with a better understanding of the decision-making process behind every mortgage and line-of-credit application. And if you've learned how to make some changes that can ease your cash flow strains, and how to save money on your borrowing costs, select the right mortgage, and pay down your debt faster, then reading this book has been time well spent. We wish you all the best in your homeownership experience. It's a milestone.

Appendix A

The House-hunting Checklist

Make a list that starts with features and then describes in each column what you need, want, don't want, and can live with. It starts to bring clarity to those features that are most important, and the others with which you're more flexible. We have found this to be a helpful exercise to have completed before you go out house hunting in earnest. Checking out some open houses starts to help identify what you want on your list and brings focus to your search. We have filled in this table with some ideas, but since everyone is different, you need to fill in what makes sense for you, whether it is a hip urban loft or a suburban detached home with a yard. For example, Roberta has a model train track in her backyard, and while it offers an occasional noise distraction, it also offers entertainment for children. And train enthusiasts seem to be numerous. We also know people who thought that having their backyard adjacent to a park was ideal, but then found the constant noise from the skating rink and tennis courts a nuisance. So before you buy, try to decide what's right for you.

	Need	Want/ Dream about	Don't want	Can live with
House Features				
Type and size of home	Single-family dwelling or condo or townhouse?	Spacious detached house	Lots of stairs to climb with huge piles of laundry	Some stairs
Bedroom configuration	Three bedrooms	Prefer all bedrooms on the same floor	Bedrooms in the basement	Master suite on separate floor from other bedrooms

	Need	Want/ Dream about	Don't want	Can live with
Other room requirements	Two bathrooms & family room	Main floor powder room & second floor laundry room & a study & playroom	One bathroom No play space	Laundry in the basement Casual living room with no playroom
Age of house and repair requirements New home or older home?	Minor decorating work	New home with fresh start and ability to choose brick colour or older home of historical significance	Gut to the studs and rebuild	Surgically focused renovations that can be done while living in the house
Property				
	Outdoor area for barbecue	Low mainten- ance garden or balcony/ terrace	High maintenance garden	Garden service
Parking features	Parking	Attached or underground garage	Street permit parking or shared driveway	"Pad" parking in front yard
Neighbourhood				
New development or more established area	A relatively established and well- maintained neighbourhood	An established neighbourhood with large lots and well- kept properties	New develop- ment with ongoing construction (mud and dust)	A developing neighbour- hood
Demo- graphics of neighbours	Need young community with play- mates for children or more adult-oriented community	A street full of young children and little traffic	Transient neighbours with no stake in the community	A mixed community with some young families
School	School within walking distance	Highest- ranked school on the next block	Drive to school	School bus

	Need	Want/ Dream about	Don't want	Can live with
Street features	Sidewalk and low traffic	Mature trees on a dead-end street with only local traffic	High traffic	Developing community
Recreational services	Park	Community Centre	No park or services	A park within a 10-minute walk
Transportation	Access to highways to get to work, and easy access to public transit	Walking distance to work, school and public transportation, along with quick highway access	A commute from work, school and inconvenient access to routes which have heavy traffic	Drive to highways and public transit within 5-10 minutes
Security	Low crime rate, strong sense of community	Being able to leave doors unlocked	Constant threat of break-ins	An alarm system
Cost to service ... Consider not only your own property, but also shared features, like boulevard gardens	Affordable cost of utilities, which can be startlingly different across regions	Well-maintained community with reasonable shared costs	Any shared costs	Premium-priced maintenance services
Access to amenities	Convenient access to grocery shopping	Close to dentist, doctor and ability to walk to convenience store	Drive to everything	Drive to most things within five minutes
Noise	Low noise issues	Tranquil and quiet	High traffic din, train, airport or other ongoing disturbance	Intermittent clamour like barking dogs

Appendix B

Monthly Expense Review	Current monthly	Expected monthly
Rent/mortgage	$	$
Municipal property tax		
Insurance		
Life insurance (mortgage life insurance or other type of life insurance)		
Medical/health insurance		
Property insurance		
Car insurance		
Utilities		
Electricity		
Gas, propane		
Water		
Telephone (land based + cell phone)		
Cable/satellite/Internet		
Home maintenance contracts including lawn care, snow removal, security		
Transportation		
Public transit pass, taxis		
Car loan payments		
Car service/licence fees		
Car maintenance, gas, oil, car washes		
Payments		
Loans and lines of credit		
Credit cards		
Other		
Grocery store		
Liquor and beer store		

Meals out		
Drugstore, including prescriptions		
Family health: dental checkups, expenses not covered by insurance plans		
Laundry: including dry cleaning, alterations and repairs		
Clothing, shoes		
Home maintenance, furniture, gardening		
Childcare, including babysitting, child support		
Gifts		
Charitable donations		
Entertainment: movies, concerts, video or DVD rentals		
Reading: books, newspapers, magazines		
Personal care including haircuts		
Pet care		
Misc: photo development, computer software		
Vacation		
Education (for anyone in the household, including tuition and supplies)		
Cash		
Interest charges and bank fees		
Savings (RRSP, RESP, other)		
Total monthly expenses		
Total monthly income		
Difference		

Appendix C

Quick Summary Checklist

You may have read the book with a high-lighter in your hand, and now you're wishing you had a quick reference summary to keep all of this information top of mind as you work through the home-buying process. Here is that quick summary:

1. Decide where your home fits in your life.
   - Start with location, location, location. Choose your neighbourhood.
   - Consider the house features that are important to you.
   - Think about the features of the property that you need and want.

2. Decide what you can afford.
   - Figure out how much money you have ready for a down payment.
   - Do some quick calculation on what you think your closing costs will be and have that amount of money ready. You can get help from your real estate agent and lender and lawyer to confirm your calculations.
   - Figure out the size of monthly mortgage payments you can afford. Use the Scotiabank "How much will my mortgage payments be?" calculator available at **www.scotiabank.com.**
   - Add up the overall carrying cost of the house, along with your regular expenses so that you can do the things you want to do. Use the list in Appendix B.

3. Figure out what you need to help you look for your home and make an offer.
   - Talk to family and friends about the real estate agent they used to get referrals, and meet real estate agents at open houses in the neighbourhood you like.
   - From a lender, get a pre-approved mortgage.
   - A lawyer is needed for purchase transactions. If you don't have a lawyer, your lender or real estate agent may be able to make a referral.
   - You will need an appraiser and home inspector when you find the home you like.
   - A property insurer is normally required as a condition of advancing the funds of the mortgage. Property insurance is arranged after your offer has been accepted, and the policy is arranged in advance of the closing date.

Glossary

Amortization Period   The actual number of years it will take to repay a mortgage loan in full. This may go beyond the term of the loan. For example, mortgages often have five-year terms, but 25-year amortization periods.

Appraisal   The process of determining the estimated value of real estate, including land and buildings.

Appraised Value   The estimated value of the property offered as security for a mortgage loan. This appraisal is done for mortgage lending purposes and may determine that the appraised value is less than the purchase price of the property.

Bond   A bond is a debt with a promise to repay the principal of that debt, along with interest. Bonds are issued by governments and large business. They can be bought and sold through bond markets on behalf of retail and institutional investors. In Canada, interest income from bonds held by an individual is taxed at your marginal tax rate.

Bridge Loan   A specialized borrowing solution for customers buying a new home before they have closed on the sale of an existing home; it's a short-term loan to carry both properties temporarily.

Closing Costs   In the broadest terms, these are all the costs associated with closing on the purchase of real estate. They can be significant, are often underestimated by homebuyers, and vary by province. The most significant component of closing costs is usually the land transfer tax. But closing costs can also include "adjustments" that are settled between the purchaser and seller, including property taxes and utility bills. Other costs involved with closing are legal fees or title insurance, the inspection cost on an existing house, survey costs, GST on a new house, appraisal fees, and mortgage registration fees.

Closing Date   The date on which the sale of the property becomes final and the new owner takes possession.

Conditional Offer A legally binding document that sets out an offer to purchase, including the conditions that must be satisfied before the offer can become a binding contract. Conditions may include the requirement of passing home inspection, availability of financing, or inclusion of certain specified items. There is normally a time limit placed on meeting the conditions. If conditions are not met by the stipulated time, then the offer expires. With an unconditional offer, if the purchaser finds that they need to retract the offer, then they will forfeit their deposit.

Cost of Borrowing The purpose of the federal government's Cost of Borrowing legislation, implemented in September 2001, was to provide consistent information to consumers, allowing for comparison shopping of interest rates from one lender to another, and from one borrowing option to another. It requires disclosure of fees and interest and penalties, expressed as an annual percentage rate (APR).

Credit Bureau An organization that provides accurate and relevant information to credit grantors for risk assessment. Full credit reports and credit scoring models are used by credit grantors, who rely on the information in credit reports or a credit score before they offer credit.

Foreclosure The legal process in which the ownership of the property is transferred to the lender if the mortgagor (borrower) does not make his mortgage payments. You may also hear the expression "power of sale," which means that the lender is requiring the sale of the property where the borrower has defaulted on his payments.

Guarantors While "co-borrowers" have equal access to the borrowing account, guarantors do not have access to the account, but share the responsibility for repayment. Essentially, your role in any borrowing is the same if you sign the documents ensuring that repayment will be made. Be very careful before you guarantee a loan for anyone, and be prepared to make repayments in the event that the primary borrower does not fulfill that responsibility.

Insurance

Creditor Insurance An insurance policy that pays out your borrowing balances (credit card, bank loan, line of credit, or mortgage) should you become critically ill or seriously injured in an accident, or die.

Mortgage Default Insurance   Also called mortgage loan insurance. Your mortgage lender is required to have this insurance if you have a high loan-to-value ratio mortgage (where the mortgage balance is greater than 75% of the value of the property).

Mortgage Life Insurance   A life insurance policy that pays out your mortgage balance in full if you die. You purchase it through your mortgage lender.

Property Insurance   A general term used to describe all types of home insurance. Most standard policies will provide coverage for damage to your home (and most personal possessions in your home) caused by theft, fire and lightning, smoke, frozen pipes, ice and snow. It can also provide other personal liability coverage. Property insurance is normally required as a condition of having a mortgage.

Title Insurance   An insurance policy that protects both you and your mortgage lender from title defects and problems, should an up-to-day survey and title search through the provincial land registry system reveal them. Since a current survey may not be available for homes in many long-established neighbourhoods or rural areas, title insurance may be accepted in place of a survey or a lawyer's search. The option to use title insurance is best made with your lawyer and simply involves a trade-off analysis of cost and time.

Interest

Annual Percentage Rate (APR)   The yearly cost of your borrowing account. For a mortgage, it will include the cost of interest and the associated fees, expressed as a percentage.

Compound Interest and Simple Interest   Interest is the charge applied for borrowing money. Simple interest is a straightforward calculation of your principal owing multiplied by your interest rate multiplied then by the expected number of years required for repayment. With compound interest, the formula is reset at the end of each designated period disclosed in your borrowing documentation. The less frequent the compounding period, the lower your overall interest cost.

Fixed Rates and Variable Rates   A fixed-rate mortgage is where the rate of interest is fixed for a specific term. A variable-rate mortgage is where the rate of interest changes as money market conditions change, usually not more than once a month. The monthly payment stays the same for a specified period; however, the amount applied towards the principal changes according to the changes (if any) in the rate of interest.

Prime Rate   This is the rate that banks charge their most creditworthy customers on borrowing. It is a variable rate, which can fluctuate up or down at any time. It is set in direct relation to the Bank of Canada rate.

Rate Blending   If you're moving, you can combine your mortgage balance outstanding on the home you're leaving with any new additional financing at a blended interest rate. Some lenders offer this service with no interest rate penalty or administration fees.

Mortgagee   Lender

Mortgagor   Borrower

Mortgage types

Assumable Mortgage   Your lender may authorize a new homeowner to take over your mortgage on a property you are selling, subject to meeting qualifying criteria. This is an attractive option if you have taken a long-term mortgage at lower than current rates, and you will no longer need a mortgage when the house is sold. By having the new homeowner assume your mortgage, they get a good rate, and you avoid early repayment charges.

Chattel Mortgage   A loan that is secured by assets other than real estate.

Closed and Open   A closed mortgage agreement does not provide for payout before maturity. A lender may permit payout under certain circumstances but will levy a penalty charge for doing so. An open mortgage provides for pre-payment or repayment at any time without penalty.

Collateral Mortgage   A mortgage loan that is secured by real property and that uses a "promissory note" for repayment.

Conventional Mortgage   A mortgage loan that does not exceed 75% of the lesser of the appraised value or the purchase price of the property. A mortgage that exceeds that limit must be insured.

High-ratio Mortgage   A mortgage where the loan amount exceeds 75% of the lesser of the appraised value or the purchase price of the property. A high-ratio mortgage must be insured by the Canada Mortgage and Housing Corporation (CMHC), the corporation of the federal government that administers the National Housing Act and provides mortgage insurance to lenders, or by a private insurer such as Genworth Financial.

Leasehold Mortgage   A mortgage on a home where the building is on leased (rented) land. The lender takes an interest in the lease.

Portable or Transferable Mortgage   A mortgage that can be transferred by the homeowner from one house to the next if you move. You can take your existing mortgage balance with you at the same interest rate for the remainder of its term, even if rates are higher.

Reverse Mortgage   An arrangement in which a homeowner borrows against the equity in their home and receives payment from the lender. The repayment of the loan is generally made when the home is sold (by the homeowner or the estate, when the homeowner passes away).

Second Mortgage   An additional mortgage on a property that already has a first mortgage. The rights of the mortgagee providing the second mortgage take priority behind the rights of the lender of the first mortgage. Some homeowners have their "mortgage" account set up as the first mortgage, and a home-equity-secured line of credit is set up as a second mortgage.

P.I.T.   Regular mortgage payments of principal, interest, and taxes.

Pre-approval   A pre-qualifying process with your lender that lets you know exactly how much financing you should be able to arrange for a home. This helps you focus your house hunting to properties in your price range. When you receive a pre-approval for your mortgage, your interest rate is usually guaranteed for a period of time from the application date.

Pre-payment   To pay more than your regularly scheduled mortgage payment.

Pre-payment Charge   A fee charged by the lender when the borrower pays off all or a portion of a mortgage more quickly than provided for in the mortgage agreement.

Renew   To extend a mortgage agreement with the same lender for another term. The length of the term and the conditions (such as the rate of interest) may be changed. Early renewal is to extend the mortgage agreement prior to the conclusion of the existing term.

Secured Debt   When borrowing is "secured" it means that you have pledged collateral against the loan. If you are unable to make your loan payment, then your lender has the right to use the "security" to help recover their loss. Collateral can include property, securities (i.e. stocks, bonds, investment accounts), durable goods (i.e. cars, boats) and other assets.

Term   The duration of a mortgage agreement. As the amortization period is longer than the term, mortgage payments made may not fully cover the outstanding principal by the end of the term.

Title   The condition by which one holds ownership of land with rights to occupy and use that land and the buildings on it exclusively.

Total Debt Service Ratio (TDSR) & Gross Debt Service Ratio (GDSR)   The TDSR is the percentage of gross annual income required to cover payments associated with housing and all other debts and obligations, such as payments on a car loan. The TDSR should not normally exceed 40% of the gross income. The GDSR is the percentage of gross annual income required to cover payments associated with housing (mortgage principal and interest, taxes, secondary financing, heating, and 50% of condominium fees, if any). The GDSR should not exceed 32% of gross annual income. For self-employed/commission sales applicants, net income is used for GDSR and TDSR ratio calculations.

Unsecured debt   When borrowing is granted by a lender without the commitment by the borrower of any collateral.

Selected Web Sites

Canada Custom and Revenue Agency   **www.ccra-adrc.gc.ca**
Use the search engine on this site to find information about the RRSP Home Buyer's plan.

Canadian Bankers Association   **www.cba.ca/en/consumer.asp**
Select the mortgage icon for information on a broad range of credit products.

Canadian Home Builders Association   **www.chba.ca**
This site provides tools to help you through the process of buying a new home, or renovating. There is guidance on how to choose your builder and get reference checks.

Canadian Mortgage and Housing Corporation   **www.cmhc-schl.gc.ca**
Canada Mortgage and Housing Corporation (CMHC) was established as a Crown corporation in 1946. CMHC's mandate is to promote the construction, repair, and modernization of housing, the improvement of living conditions, housing affordability, and choice. Their web site offers a wide range of information for home buyers and homeowners.

Canadian Real Estate Association   **www.crea.ca**
The CREA represents realtors across Canada and provides the Realtor *Code of Ethics* along with guidance for both home buyers and home sellers.

Credit Counselling Canada   **www.creditcounsellingcanada.ca**
This site connects you to not-for-profit credit counselling agencies, which provide assistance to borrowers who are experiencing problems with their debt, and helps people learn how to use their credit wisely. In Ontario, go to **www.indebt.org** for the Ontario Association of Credit Counselling Services (OACCS).

Equifax Canada Inc.   **www.equifax.ca**
Equifax provides consumer information about credit reporting and how to get a copy of your own credit report to ensure it is accurate.

First Canadian Title   **www.firstcanadiantitle.com**
First Canadian Title Company Limited and its parent, First American Title Insurance Company, together form Canada's leading provider of title insurance. This web site explains what title insurance is and the range of real estate-related products and services they offer.

Genworth Financial (formerly GEMICO)   **www.genworth.com**

Under Products and Services, select Mortgage Insurance, then click on the Canadian site for homebuyer information, including a guide to figure out how much your mortgage default insurance may cost.

Insurance Bureau of Canada   **www.ibc.ca**

A helpful resource with information about different types of policies for insuring your home and its contents.

Multiple Listing Service   **www.mls.ca**

The MLS system is a trademarked service of the Canadian Real Estate Association. It provides information on properties currently listed for sale or rent in the Canadian market.

Scotiabank   **www.scotiabank.com**

In addition to information on products and services mentioned in the book, on this site, you'll find a few quick ways to help you lower your borrowing costs and find the money you didn't know you had.

The Renovation Roadmap   **www.myhomereno.com**

This web site was launched in 2001 by the Canadian Home Builders Association to provide renovation advice and information to Canadian consumers. The site includes information and tools to help you frame your renovation plan, including how to set goals, how to make your home healthier and more energy-efficient, and how to find the right professional contractor.

TransUnion Canada   **www.tuc.ca**

TransUnion's "credit learning centre" provides answers to many questions on credit, along with the ability to order your own credit profile.

Selected References

Adams, Michael. *Better Happy Than Rich? Canadians, Money and the Meaning of Life.* Toronto: Viking, 2000.

Canadian Mortgage and Housing Corporation. *2003 Canadian Housing Observer.*

Hamilton, Sheryl. "The Home of the Future, Then and Now." *Canadian Home Economics Journal* 52: Spring 2003.

Ipsos Reid–Scotiabank consumer credit poll, October 2003.

Kshirsagar, Alok E., Paul G. McNamara, and Janette Weir. "A Broadband Future for Financial Advice." *The McKinsey Quarterly* 2: 2001.

Rybczynski, Witold. *Home: A Short History of an Idea.* Toronto: Viking, 1986.

Warren, Adrienne. Special Report: "An Assessment of North American Household Balance Sheets." Scotiabank Group Global Economic Research, January 2004.

Watkins, Trevor. "The Origin of House and Home." *World Archaeology* 21: Feb 1990.

Acknowledgements

Canadians, and in particular our customers, have been telling us their personal stories and dreams over many years. We have heard your worries and shared your celebrations. Listening to you has given us much of the insight that was needed to frame this book. Thank you to all the Scotiabank customers who have ever participated in research and shared your perspective and experience. You are our inspiration.

We are grateful to all the support we have received from everyone on the Scotiabank team. We want to single out the effort made every day by Scotiabank's personal bankers across the country, helping our customers be better borrowers.

We are indebted to colleagues, family, and friends who have read and re-read our various drafts and given us comments. In particular, Rick White, Ain Saaliste, Gillian Riley, Lisa Ritchie, Tracey Marshall, David Scott, and Kim Karges. Thank you to those who checked and re-checked the facts: Ron Cheong, Cristian Mandachescu, Jeannie Melardi, Jeffrey Murray, Tara Rodgers, and Teresa Shih. And, thank you to Charles Lambert, Paul Lamothe, Liz Ross, and David Stafford for your reviews. Thank you to Laura Ellis for your research effort, to Scott Galbraith at GE Mortgage Insurance, John Wright at Ipsos-Reid, and Pooneh Baghai at McKinsey for your professional perspective. And thank you to Andrea Hopson for sharing your deliberations.

Let's give credit where it is due: It was really Anna Porter of Key Porter Books who got the ball rolling when she was looking for guidance to help a family member in the process of buying a house and found few resources. The idea evolved from there. Anna has been tremendously supportive throughout this process and a great inspiration to us.

And since writers are only as effective as their editors, you'll enjoy reading this book all the more since it has been through the hands of Meg Taylor. Thanks to the whole publishing team at Key Porter, especially Lyn Cadence, Brad Kalbfleisch, and Peter Maher.

To our families, our lifelines: You make us want to make you proud. Thank you for your support and enthusiastic encouragement and patience. We tackled the project of writing this book outside of our already hectic work lives, and you have given us the time we needed to see this through. Our sincere thanks to each of you.

Index